Books by Abraham Joshua Heschel

THE WISDOM OF HESCHEL
A PASSION FOR TRUTH
ISRAEL: AN ECHO OF ETERNITY
THE INSECURITY OF FREEDOM
WHO IS MAN?
THEOLOGY OF ANCIENT JUDAISM
[two volumes]
THE SABBATH
THE EARTH IS THE LORD'S
MAN'S QUEST FOR GOD
GOD IN SEARCH OF MAN
MAN IS NOT ALONE
MAIMONIDES
ABRAVANEL
THE QUEST FOR CERTAINTY IN SAADIA'S PHILOSOPHY
THE PROPHETS
MORAL GRANDEUR AND SPIRITUAL AUDACITY

THE SABBATH

the S A B B

ABRAHAM JOSHUA HESCHEL WITH
WOOD ENGRAVINGS BY ILYA SCHOR
FARRAR, STRAUS AND GIROUX
NEW YORK

A T H

its meaning for modern man

Farrar, Straus and Giroux
19 Union Square West, New York 10003

Library of Congress Control Number: 2005926224
ISBN-13: 978-0-374-52975-8
ISBN-10: 0-374-52975-2

Designed by Marshall Lee

www.fsgbooks.com

10 9 8 7 6 5 4 3

CONTENTS

Introduction

by Susannah Heschel

When my father raised his kiddush cup on Friday evenings, closed his eyes, and chanted the prayer sanctifying the wine, I always felt a rush of emotion. As he chanted with an old, sacred family melody, he blessed the wine and the Sabbath with his prayer, and I also felt he was blessing my life and that of everyone at the table. I treasured those moments.

Friday evenings in my home were the climax of the week, as they are for every religious Jewish family. My mother and I kindled the lights for the Sabbath, and all of a sudden I felt transformed, emotionally and even physically. After lighting the candles in the dining room, we would walk into the living room, which had windows overlooking the Hudson River, facing west, and we would marvel at the sunset that soon arrived.

The sense of peace that came upon us as we kindled the lights was created, in part, by the hectic tension of Fridays. Preparation for a holy day, my father often said, was as important as the day itself. During the busy mornings my mother shopped for groceries, and in the afternoons the atmosphere grew increasingly nervous as she cooked. My father came home from his office an hour or two before sunset to take care of his own preparations, and as the last minutes of the workweek came close, both of my parents were in the kitchen, frantically trying to remember what they might have forgotten to prepare—Had the kettle boiled? Was the *blech* covering the stove? Was the oven turned on?

Then, suddenly, it was time: twenty minutes before sunset. Whatever hadn't been finished in the kitchen we simply left behind as we lit the candles and blessed the arrival of the Sabbath. My father writes, "The Sabbath comes like a caress, wiping away fear, sorrow and somber memories."

My father rarely went to the synagogue on Friday evenings, preferring to pray at home, and our dinners were usually quiet, slow, and relaxed. My parents did not socialize very much, but every two months or so they would invite a few friends or colleagues to Shabbat dinner. The meal was always the same: our challahs came from our local bakery, and my mother made chicken soup, roast cornish hen, salad, and vegetables. For dessert, my father would peel a Golden Delicious apple, trying to keep the peel in one piece, and we would share apple chunks. My mother was not an enthusiastic cook and my father was always on a salt-free diet, so the food was not thrilling. Still, at the beginning of every meal, my father lifted his fork, looked at me, and said, "Mommy is a good cook."

We had one unusual custom at our Shabbat table: my father had received a gift from his brother-in-law, the Kopycznitzer Rebbe, of two long, braided silver spice holders, in which he kept myrtle and eucalyptus leaves. Although scented spices are usually blessed and smelled at havdalah, as Shabbat ends, we would bless and smell the spices just before kiddush, the prayer over the wine, in a Hasidic custom based on a rabbinic passage that my father discusses in *The Sabbath*.

When we had guests for dinner, they were nearly always academic refugees from Europe, and the conversation at the table was always focused on Europe. Invariably, they talked about German scholars they had known: Jews who had fled to the U.S. or Israel, others who had perished. They did not talk about the murder process of the Holocaust, nor did they use that word in those days, but they would talk about the non-Jewish scholars who had been exposed as Nazis in Max Weinreich's book *Hitler's Professors*. Like my father, most of my parent's friends had studied before the war at German universities and they remained shocked, twenty and thirty years after the war ended, that scholars whose work they had admired had become Nazis. German culture always colored those conversations. I grew up hearing about Goethe and Heine, Schopenhauer and Husserl, long before I read Hawthorne, Melville, Emerson, or Thoreau in school. Given the cultural world of my parents' home, I have always had a sense of being a tourist in America.

Just as often, the conversation centered on Eastern Europe, on the Hasidic world my father had come from. He loved to tell his guests stories about various Hasidic rebbes, or describe teachings from Hasidic texts. Few of my parents' friends came from that world, but for my father, the Sabbath was always a return to the Sabbaths of his youth and memories of his family and friends.

Indeed, on the Sabbath my father's reading habits shifted. He did not read secular books, works of philosophy or politics, but instead turned to Hebrew religious texts. Because writing is forbidden on the Sabbath, he would sometimes place a napkin or a paper clip to mark a page, so that years later I could tell which books had been his Shabbat reading. Those books brought him back each Sabbath to stories of his childhood and to the feeling that he had grown up surrounded by people of "religious nobility." (Something of a corresponding situation existed at one time with the French edition of *The Sabbath*, which was published in France under the title *Les Bâttiseurs du Temps* [Architecture in Time]. According to his letters, the great poet Paul Celan kept a copy of my father's book on his bedside table toward the end of his life.)

On Shabbat morning we attended services at the Jewish Theological Seminary, where my father taught, and in the congregation sat faculty and students from the seminary and from Columbia University. It was an Orthodox service, conducted entirely in Hebrew, and men and women sat separately. Many weeks we heard a sermon delivered by a graduating rabbinical student, and on the walk home from the synagogue faculty members commented, often severely, on the quality of the sermon. The walk took only fifteen minutes, but my father had a habit of taking a few steps, then stopping to talk over a point before moving on, so that the walk often lasted half an hour. When I was small, he sometimes carried me on his shoulders, and as I grew older, his colleagues helped him entertain me.

Shabbat lunch was informal and lighthearted, a time for joking and teasing. After lunch my parents took their weekly nap, followed by tea and a walk in Riverside Park, across the street. There we would meet friends and colleagues taking their Shabbat afternoon strolls.

There are really two kinds of Shabbat experiences: those of the fall and winter months, when the Sabbath begins around four o'clock on Friday afternoons and ends around five o'clock on Saturday, and those of the spring and summer, when the Sabbath starts at eight or eight-thirty and ends at nine o'clock or even later. In the winter months, our Friday nights continued long after dinner as my parents sat at the table, drinking tea and reading. During the spring months, the long Shabbat afternoons became the peaceful and quiet focus of the day.

Often my parents would invite students for a Shabbat afternoon high tea. My mother served cheese and crackers, various cakes, sometimes even a magnificent *Herrentorte*—a loaf of bread sliced lengthwise and filled with layers of various kinds of fish and egg salads and frosted with a cream-cheese-and-anchovy spread. My father was attentive to each student, asking about his studies, hometown rabbis, and goals for the future. As the afternoon turned dusky, he offered each one a Siddur, to pray the evening service. Together we made havdalah, the prayer concluding Shabbat, and then the students departed.

Sunday was once again a weekday. During the winter months, my father sometimes taught on Sunday mornings, and my mother was at her piano, practicing. Nearly every summer, however, my parents rented a house in Los Angeles, to be near my mother's brothers and their families. The houses were occasionally too far from a synagogue to walk, so friends would come to my parents' home for services on Shabbat morning. My mother would prepare a light kiddush for everyone, and guests stayed well into the afternoon. By the time the Sabbath ended on Saturday night, it was late and we went to sleep. Sunday mornings became the post-Shabbat moments of transition as my father went to his study and my mother to her piano. Sunday afternoons in the summer were filled with music: we would go to the home of my mother's brother, a physician who played the violin. He had a large music room with two pianos, and his friends would arrange themselves in trios, quartets, and quintets, and spend the day playing chamber music. The house had a large swimming pool just outside the music room, and my father and I would float in the water, read a book, and listen to the music while my mother played.

At the time *The Sabbath* was published, in 1951, my father had been in the United States for only eleven years. When he had arrived in 1940, his English had been weak, but he mastered the language remarkably quickly and went on to write in an extraordinarily rich and poetic style. Indeed, my parents would often laugh because early readers of the book couldn't imagine my father was the author—they thought my mother had ghostwritten it! The book's language is intrinsic to its meaning; its elegiac, poetic tone evokes the mood of the Sabbath that he describes.

The Sabbath appeared at a time when American Jews were assimilating radically and when many were embarrassed by public expressions of Jewishness. Even among rabbis and Jewish leaders, a rejection of Jewish mysticism, Hasidism, and even of theology and spirituality was common. It was as if they desired a religionless Judaism—a Judaism without God, faith, or belief. For them, the Sabbath interfered with jobs, socializing, shopping, and simply being American.

In trying to reintroduce the importance of the Sabbath, my father did not berate Jews for their neglect of religious observance, nor did he demand obedience to Jewish law based on the absolute authority of rabbinic texts. Writing in an era in which books by clergy advocating the psychological health promoted by religion were coming into vogue, my father went against the trend. He insisted that the Sabbath is not about psychology or sociology; it doesn't serve to make us calmer or to hold the family together. Nor does the Sabbath represent a rejection of modernity or the secular world—for him, the Sabbath was a complement to building civilization, not a withdrawal from it. In contrast to more recent approaches to the Sabbath, my father did not emphasize the importance of "ritual" (he believed that the words "customs" and "ceremonies" should be eradicated from the Jewish vocabulary), nor did he view the Sabbath as a vehicle for solidifying Jewish continuity.

Yet my father's approach to the Sabbath did reflect some of the political concerns and language of the day; the themes of freedom and liberty recur in the book. He writes that we need the Sabbath in order to survive civilization: "Gallantly, ceaselessly, quietly, man must fight for inner liberty" to remain independent of the enslavement of the material world. "Inner liberty depends upon being exempt from domination of things as well as from domination of people. There are many who have acquired a high degree of political and social liberty, but only very few are not enslaved to things. This is our constant problem—how to live with people and remain free, how to live with things and remain independent."

My father defines Judaism as a religion centrally concerned with holiness in time. Some religions build great cathedrals or temples, but Judaism constructs the Sabbath as an architecture of time. Creating holiness in time requires a different sensibility than building a cathedral in space: "We must conquer space in order to sanctify time." My father did not mean to imply, as some have suggested, a denigration of space or a denial of the significance of the land of Israel. His commitment to Israel and its sanctity is attested to in his book *Israel: An Echo of Eternity*. In the cases of both the Sabbath and Israel, he emphasizes that sanctification is dependent upon human behavior and attitude. Sanctifying the Sabbath is part of our imitation of God, but it also becomes a way to find God's presence. It is not in space but in time, he writes, that we find God's likeness. In the Bible, no thing or place is holy by itself; not even the Promised Land is called holy. While the holiness of the land and of festivals depends on the actions of the Jewish people, who have to sanctify them, the holiness of the Sabbath, he writes, preceded the holiness of Israel. Even if people fail to observe the Sabbath, it remains holy.

How do we bring about the elusive atmosphere that is the Sabbath? Sanctity is a quality, my father emphasized, that we create. We know what to do with space, but how do we shape sacred time? Six days a week we live with a fury of acquisitiveness, he writes; Shabbat renews the soul and we rediscover who we are. "The Sabbath is the presence of God in the world, open to the soul of man." God is not in things of space, but in moments of time. How do we perceive God's presence? There are some helpful Sabbath laws—those that require shutting off secular demands and refraining from work. In enumerating the categories that constitute "work," the Mishnah describes types of activities necessary to build technological civilization. Yet my father goes further. Not only is it forbidden to light a fire on the Sabbath, but, he writes, "Ye shall kindle no fire— not even the fire of righteous indignation." In our home, certain topics were avoided on the Sabbath— politics, the Holocaust, the war in Vietnam—while others were emphasized. Observing the Sabbath is not only about refraining from work, but about creating *menuha*, a restfulness that is also a celebration. The Sabbath is a day for body as well as soul. It is a sin to be sad on the Sabbath, a lesson my father often repeated and always observed.

With the Sabbath comes a miracle: the soul is resurrected, an additional soul arrives, and the effulgence of Sabbath holiness fills every corner of the household.

Anger is lifted, tensions are gone, and there is a glow on the face.

Creating Shabbat begins with a sense of longing. Strikingly, my father turns our expectations around. It is not we who long for a day of rest, but the Sabbath spirit that is lonely and longs for us. We are the mate of the Sabbath, and each week, through our sanctification of the Sabbath, we marry the day. That marriage shapes us: "What *we are* depends on what *the Sabbath is* to us." Similarly, the Sabbath does not simply come into being on Saturdays; the depth of its experience is created, he writes, by how we behave on the other six days of the week; they are a pilgrimage to the Sabbath.

Shabbat comes with its own holiness; we enter not simply a day, but an atmosphere. My father cites the Zohar: the Sabbath is the name of God. We are within the Sabbath rather than the Sabbath being within us. For my father, the question is how to perceive that holiness: not how *much* to observe, but *how* to observe. Strict adherence to the laws regulating Sabbath observance doesn't suffice; the goal is creating the Sabbath as a foretaste of paradise. The Sabbath is a metaphor for paradise and a testimony to God's presence; in our prayers, we anticipate a messianic era that will be a Sabbath, and each Shabbat prepares us for that experience: "Unless one learns how to relish the taste of Sabbath . . . one will be unable to enjoy the taste of eternity in the world to come." It was on the seventh day that God gave the world a soul, and "[the world's] survival depends upon the holiness of the seventh day." The task, he writes, becomes how to convert time into eternity, how to fill our time with spirit: "Six days a week we wrestle with the world, wringing profit from the earth; on the Sabbath we especially care for the seed of eternity planted in the soul. The world has our hands, but our soul belongs to Someone Else."

On my father's last Shabbat we had a wonderful dinner with many friends, after which one of our guests read aloud some of my father's Yiddish poems, written when he was a young man. He went to sleep that night and never woke. In Jewish tradition, dying in one's sleep is called a kiss of God, and dying on the Sabbath is a gift that is merited by piety. For the pious person, my father once wrote, it is a privilege to die.

SUSANNAH HESCHEL holds the Eli Black Chair in Jewish Studies at Dartmouth College. She is the author of *Abraham Geiger and the Jewish Jesus* (University of Chicago) and *The Aryan Jesus: Christians, Nazis, and the Bible* (Princeton) as well as the coeditor, with Robert P. Ericksen, of *Betrayal: German Churches and the Holocaust* (Augsburg Fortress Publishers), among other books.

Prologue

זכור את יום השבת לקדשו

Architecture of Time

Technical civilization is man's conquest of space. It is a triumph frequently achieved by sacrificing an essential ingredient of existence, namely, time. In technical civilization, we expend time to gain space. To enhance our power in the world of space is our main objective. Yet to have more does not mean to be more. The power we attain in the world of space terminates abruptly at the borderline of time. But time is the heart of existence.[1]

To gain control of the world of space is certainly one of our tasks. The danger begins when in gaining power in the realm of space we forfeit all aspirations in the realm of time. There is a realm of time where the goal is not to have but to be, not to own but to give, not to control but to share, not to subdue but to be in accord. Life goes wrong when the control of space, the acquisition of things of space, becomes our sole concern.

Nothing is more useful than power, nothing more frightful. We have often suffered from degradation by poverty, now we are threatened with degradation through power. There is happiness in the love of labor, there is misery in the love of gain. Many hearts and pitchers are broken at the fountain of profit. Selling himself into slavery to things, man becomes a utensil that is broken at the fountain.

Technical civilization stems primarily from the desire of man to subdue and manage the forces of nature. The manufacture of tools, the art of spinning and farming, the building of houses, the craft of sailing—all this goes on in man's spatial surroundings. The mind's preoccupation with things of space affects, to this day, all activities of man. Even religions are frequently dominated by the notion that the deity resides in space, within particular localities like mountains, forests, trees or stones, which are, therefore, singled out as holy places; the deity is bound to a particular land; holiness a quality associated with things of space, and the primary question is: Where is the god? There is much enthusiasm for the idea that God is present in the universe, but that idea is taken to mean His presence in space rather than in time, in nature rather than in history; as if He were a thing, not a spirit.

Even pantheistic philosophy is a religion of space: the Supreme Being is thought to be the infinite space. *Deus sive natura* has extension, or space, as its attribute, not time; time to Spinoza is merely an accident of motion, a mode of thinking. And his desire to develop a philosophy *more geometrico*, in the manner of geometry, which is the science of space, is significant of his space-mindedness.

The primitive mind finds it hard to realize an idea without the aid of imagination, and it is the realm of space where imagination wields its sway. Of the gods it must have a visible image; where there is no image, there is no god. The reverence for the sacred image, for the sacred monument or place, is not only indigenous to most religions, it has even been retained by men of all ages, all nations, pious, superstitious or even antireligious; they all continue to pay homage to banners and flags, to national shrines, to monuments erected to kings or heroes. Everywhere the desecration of holy shrines is considered a sacrilege, and the shrine may become so important that the idea it stands for is consigned to oblivion. The memorial becomes an aid to amnesia; the means stultify the end. For things of space are at the mercy of man. Though too sacred to be polluted, they are not too sacred to be exploited. To retain the holy, to perpetuate the presence of god, his image is fashioned. Yet a god who can be fashioned, a god who can be confined, is but a shadow of man.

We are all infatuated with the splendor of space, with the grandeur of things of space. Thing is a category that lies heavy on our minds, tyrannizing all our thoughts. Our imagination tends to mold all concepts in its image. In our daily lives we attend primarily to that which the senses are spelling out for us: to what the eyes perceive, to what the fingers touch. Reality to us is thinghood, consisting of substances that occupy space; even God is conceived by most of us as a thing.

The result of our thinginess is our blindness to all reality that fails to identify itself as a thing, as a matter of fact. This is obvious in our understanding of time, which, being thingless and insubstantial, appears to us as if it had no reality.[2]

Indeed, we know what to do with space but do not know what to do about time, except to make it subservient to space. Most of us seem to labor for the sake of things of space. As a result we suffer from a deeply rooted dread of time and stand aghast when compelled to look into its face.[3] Time to us is sarcasm, a slick treacherous monster with a jaw like a furnace incinerating every moment of our lives. Shrinking, therefore, from facing time, we escape for shelter to things of space. The intentions we are unable to carry out we deposit in space; possessions become the symbols of our repressions, jubilees of frustrations. But things of space are not fireproof; they only add fuel to the flames. Is the joy of possession an antidote to the terror of time which grows to be a dread of inevitable death? Things, when magnified, are forgeries of happiness, they are a threat to our very lives; we are more harassed than supported by the Frankensteins of spatial things.

It is impossible for man to shirk the problem of time. The more we think the more we realize: we cannot conquer time through space. We can only master time in time.[4]

The higher goal of spiritual living is not to amass a wealth of information, but to face sacred moments. In a religious experience, for example, it is not a thing that imposes itself on man but a spiritual presence.[5] What is retained in the soul is the moment of insight rather than the place where the act came to pass. A moment of insight is a fortune, transporting us beyond the confines of measured time. Spiritual life begins to decay when we fail to sense the grandeur of what is eternal in time.

Our intention here is not to deprecate the world of space. To disparage space and the blessing of things of space, is to disparage the works of creation, the works which God beheld and saw "it was good." The world cannot be seen exclusively *sub specie temporis*. Time and space are interrelated. To overlook either of them is to be partially blind. What we plead against is man's unconditional surrender to space, his enslavement to things. We must not forget that it is not a thing that lends significance to a moment; it is the moment that lends significance to things.

The Bible is more concerned with time than with space. It sees the world in the dimension of time. It pays more attention to generations, to events, than to countries, to things; it is more concerned with history than with geography. To understand the teaching of the Bible, one must accept its premise that time has a meaning for life which is at least equal to that of space; that time has a significance and sovereignty of its own.

There is no equivalent for the word "thing" in biblical Hebrew. The word "*davar*," which in later Hebrew came to denote thing, means in biblical Hebrew: speech; word; message; report; tidings; advice; request; promise; decision; sentence; theme, story; saying, utterance; business, occupation; acts; good deeds; events; way, manner, reason, cause; but never "thing." Is this a sign of linguistic poverty, or rather an indication of an unwarped view of the world, of not equating reality (derived from the Latin word *res*, thing) with thinghood?

One of the most important facts in the history of religion was the transformation of agricultural festivals into commemorations of historical events. The festivals of ancient peoples were intimately linked with nature's seasons. They celebrated what happened in the life of nature in the respective seasons. Thus the value of the festive day was determined by the things nature did or did not bring forth. In Judaism, Passover, originally a spring festival, became a celebration of the exodus from Egypt; the Feast of Weeks, an old harvest festival at the end of the wheat harvest (*hag hakazir*, Exodus 23:16; 34:22), became the celebration of the day on which the Torah was given at Sinai; the Feast of the Booths, an old festival of vintage (*hag haasif*, Ex. 23:16), commemorates the dwelling of the Israelites in booths during their sojourn in the wilderness (Leviticus 23:42f.). To Israel the unique events of historic time were spiritually more significant than the repetitive processes in the cycle of nature, even though physical sustenance depended on the latter. While the deities of other peoples were associated with places or things, the God of Israel was the God of events: the Redeemer from slavery, the Revealer of the Torah, manifesting Himself in events of history rather than in things or places. Thus, the faith in the unembodied, in the unimaginable was born.

Judaism is a *religion of time* aiming at *the sanctification of time.* Unlike the space-minded man to whom time is unvaried, iterative, homogeneous, to whom all hours are alike, qualitiless, empty shells, the Bible senses the diversified character of time. There are no two hours alike. Every hour is unique and the only one given at the moment, exclusive and endlessly precious.

Judaism teaches us to be attached to *holiness in time,* to be attached to sacred events, to learn how to consecrate sanctuaries that emerge from the magnificent stream of a year. The Sabbaths are our great cathedrals; and our Holy of Holies is a shrine that neither the Romans nor the Germans were able to burn; a shrine that even apostasy cannot easily obliterate: the Day of Atonement. According to the ancient rabbis, it is not the observance of the Day of Atonement, but the Day itself, the "essence of the Day," which, with man's repentance, atones for the sins of man.[6]

Jewish ritual may be characterized as the art of significant forms in time, as *architecture of time.* Most of its observances—the Sabbath, the New Moon, the festivals, the Sabbatical and the Jubilee year—depend on a certain hour of the day or season of the year. It is, for example, the evening, morning, or afternoon that brings with it the call to prayer. The main themes of faith lie in the realm of time. We remember the day of the exodus from Egypt, the day when Israel stood at Sinai; and our Messianic hope is the expectation of a day, of the end of days.

In a well-composed work of art an idea of outstanding importance is not introduced haphazardly, but, like a king at an official ceremony, it is presented at a moment and in a way that will bring to light its authority and leadership. In the Bible, words are employed with exquisite care, particularly those which, like pillars of fire, lead the way in the far-flung system of the biblical world of meaning.

One of the most distinguished words in the Bible is the word *qadosh*, holy; a word which more than any other is representative of the mystery and majesty of the divine. Now what was the first holy object in the history of the world? Was it a mountain? Was it an altar?

It is, indeed, a unique occasion at which the distinguished word *qadosh* is used for the first time: in the Book of Genesis at the end of the story of creation. How extremely significant is the fact that it is applied to time: "And God blessed the seventh *day* and made it *holy*."[7] There is no reference in the record of creation to any object in space that would be endowed with the quality of holiness.

This is a radical departure from accustomed religious thinking. The mythical mind would expect that, after heaven and earth have been established, God would create a holy place—a holy mountain or a holy spring—whereupon a sanctuary is to be established. Yet it seems as if to the Bible it is *holiness in time*, the Sabbath, which comes first.

When history began, there was only one holiness in the world, holiness in time. When at Sinai the word of God was about to be voiced, a call for holiness in *man* was proclaimed: "Thou shalt be unto me a holy people." It was only after the people had succumbed to the temptation of worshipping a thing, a golden calf, that the erection of a Tabernacle, of holiness in *space*, was commanded.[8] The sanctity of time came first, the sanctity of man came second, and the sanctity of space last. Time was hallowed by God; space, the Tabernacle, was consecrated by Moses.[9]

While the festivals celebrate events that happened in time, the date of the month assigned for each festival in the calendar is determined by the life in nature. Passover and the Feast of Booths, for example, coincide with the full moon, and the date of all festivals is a day in the month, and the month is a reflection of what goes on periodically in the realm of nature, since the Jewish month begins with the new moon, with the reappearance of the lunar crescent in the evening sky.[10] In contrast, the Sabbath is entirely independent of the month and unrelated to the moon.[11] Its date is not determined by any event in nature, such as the new moon, but by the act of creation. Thus the essence of the Sabbath is completely detached from the world of space.

The meaning of the Sabbath is to celebrate time rather than space. Six days a week we live under the tyranny of things of space; on the Sabbath we try to become attuned to *holiness in time*. It is a day on which we are called upon to share in what is eternal in time, to turn from the results of creation to the mystery of creation; from the world of creation to the creation of the world.

Part One

I

A Palace in Time

He who wants to enter the holiness of the day must first lay down the profanity of clattering commerce, of being yoked to toil. He must go away from the screech of dissonant days, from the nervousness and fury of acquisitiveness and the betrayal in embezzling his own life. He must say farewell to manual work and learn to understand that the world has already been created and will survive without the help of man. Six days a week we wrestle with the world, wringing profit from the earth; on the Sabbath we especially care for the seed of eternity planted in the soul. The world has our hands, but our soul belongs to Someone Else. Six days a week we seek to dominate the world, on the seventh day we try to dominate the self.

When the Romans met the Jews and noticed their strict adherence to the law of abstaining from labor on the Sabbath, their only reaction was contempt. The Sabbath is a sign of Jewish indolence, was the opinion held by Juvenal, Seneca and others.

In defense of the Sabbath, Philo, the spokesman of the Greek-speaking Jews of Alexandria, says: "On this day we are commanded to abstain from all work, not because the law inculcates slackness. . . . Its object is rather to give man relaxation from continuous and unending toil and by refreshing their bodies with a regularly calculated system of remissions to send them out renewed to their old activities. For a breathing spell enables not merely ordinary people but athletes also to collect their strength with a stronger force behind them to undertake promptly and patiently each of the tasks set before them." [1]

Here the Sabbath is represented not in the spirit of the Bible but in the spirit of Aristotle. According to the Stagirite, "we need relaxation, because we cannot work continuously. Relaxation, then, is not an end"; it is "for the sake of activity," for the sake of gaining strength for new efforts. [2] To the biblical mind, however, labor is the means toward an end, and the Sabbath as a day of rest, as a day of abstaining from toil, is not for the purpose of recovering one's lost strength and becoming fit for the forthcoming labor. The Sabbath is a day for the sake of life. Man is not a beast of burden, and the Sabbath is not for the purpose of enhancing the efficiency of his work. "Last in creation, first in intention," [3] the Sabbath is "the end of the creation of heaven and earth." [4]

The Sabbath is not for the sake of the weekdays; the weekdays are for the sake of Sabbath. [5] It is not an interlude but the climax of living.

Three acts of God denoted the seventh day: He rested, He blessed and He hallowed the seventh day (Genesis 2:2-3). To the prohibition of labor is, therefore, added the blessing of delight and the accent of sanctity. Not only the hands of man celebrate the day, the tongue and the soul keep the Sabbath. One does not talk on it in the same manner in which one talks on weekdays. Even thinking of business or labor should be avoided.

Labor is a craft, but perfect rest is an art. It is the result of an accord of body, mind and imagination. To attain a degree of excellence in art, one must accept its discipline, one must adjure slothfulness. The seventh

day is a *palace in time* which we build. It is made of
soul, of joy and reticence. In its atmosphere, a discipline is a reminder of adjacency to eternity. Indeed, the splendor of the day is expressed in terms of
abstentions, just as the mystery of God is more ade-
quately conveyed *via negationis,* in the categories of
negative theology which claims that we can never say
what He is, we can only say what He is not. We often
feel how poor the edifice would be were it built exclusively of our rituals and deeds which are so awk-
ward and often so obtrusive. How else express glory
in the presence of eternity, if not by the silence of abstaining from noisy acts? These restrictions utter songs
to those who know how to stay at a palace with a queen.

There is a word that is seldom said, a word for an
emotion almost too deep to be expressed: the love of
the Sabbath. The word is rarely found in our literature, yet for more than two thousand years the emotion filled our songs and moods. It was as if a whole
people were in love with the seventh day. Much of its
spirit can only be understood as an example of love
carried to the extreme. As in the chivalric poetry of the
Middle Ages, the "underlying principle was that love
should always be absolute, and that the lover's every
thought and act should on all occasions correspond
with the most extreme feelings or sentiments or fancies
possible for a lover."

"Love, with the troubadours and their ladies, was a
source of joy. Its commands and exigencies made life's
supreme law. Love was knighthood's service; it was
loyalty and devotion; it was the noblest human giving.
It was also the spring of excellence, the inspiration of
high deeds." [6] Chivalric culture created a romantic
conception of adoration and love that to this day dom-
inates in its combination of myth and passion the lit-

erature and mind of Western man. The Jewish contribution to the idea of love is the conception of love of the Sabbath, the love of a day, of spirit in the form of time.

What is so luminous about a day? What is so precious to captivate the hearts? It is because the seventh day is a mine where spirit's precious metal can be found with which to construct the palace in time, a dimension in which the human is at home with the divine; a dimension in which man aspires to approach the likeness of the divine.

For where shall the likeness of God be found? There is no quality that space has in common with the essence of God. There is not enough freedom on the top of the mountain; there is not enough glory in the silence of the sea. Yet the likeness of God can be found in time, which is eternity in disguise.

The art of keeping the seventh day is the art of painting on the canvas of time the mysterious grandeur of the climax of creation: as He sanctified the seventh day, so shall we. The love of the Sabbath is the love of man for what he and God have in common. Our keeping the Sabbath day is a paraphrase of His sanctification of the seventh day.

What would be a world without Sabbath? It would be a world that knew only itself or God distorted as a thing or the abyss separating Him from the world; a world without the vision of a window in eternity that opens into time.

For all the idealization, there is no danger of the idea of the Sabbath becoming a fairy-tale. With all the romantic idealization, the Sabbath remains a concrete fact, a legal institution and a social order. There is no danger of its becoming a disembodied spirit, for the spirit of the Sabbath must always be in accord with actual deeds, with definite actions and abstentions. The real and the spiritual are one, like body and soul in a living man. It is for the law to clear the path; it is for the soul to sense the spirit.

This is what the ancient rabbis felt: the Sabbath demands all of man's attention, the service and single-minded devotion of total love. The logic of such a conception compelled them to enlarge constantly the system of laws and rules of observance. They sought to ennoble human nature and make it worthy of being in the presence of the royal day.

Yet law and love, discipline and delight, were not always fused. In their illustrious fear of desecrating the spirit of the day, the ancient rabbis established a level of observance which is within the reach of exalted souls but not infrequently beyond the grasp of ordinary men.

The glorification of the day, the insistence upon strict observance, did not, however, lead the rabbis to a deification of the law. "The Sabbath is given unto you, not you unto the Sabbath." [7] The ancient rabbis knew that excessive piety may endanger the fulfilment of the essence of the law.[8] "There is nothing more important, according to the Torah, than to preserve human life . . . Even when there is the slightest possibility that a life may be at stake one may disregard every prohibition of the law." [9] One must sacrifice mitzvot *for the sake of man* rather than sacrifice man *"for the sake of mitzvot."* The purpose of the Torah is "to bring life to Israel, in this world and in the world to come." [10]

Continuous austerity may severely dampen, yet levity would certainly obliterate the spirit of the day. One cannot modify a precious filigree with a spear or operate on a brain with a plowshare. It must always be remembered that the Sabbath is not an occasion for diversion or frivolity; not a day to shoot fireworks or to turn somersaults, but an opportunity to mend our tattered lives; to collect rather than to dissipate time. Labor without dignity is the cause of misery; rest without spirit the source of depravity. Indeed, the prohibitions have succeeded in preventing the vulgarization of the grandeur of the day.

Two things the people of Rome anxiously desired— bread and circus games.[11] But man does not live by bread and circus games alone. Who will teach him how to desire anxiously the spirit of a sacred day?

The Sabbath is the most precious present mankind has received from the treasure house of God. All week we think: The spirit is too far away, and we succumb to spiritual absenteeism, or at best we pray: Send us a little of Thy spirit. On the Sabbath the spirit stands and pleads: Accept all excellence from me. . .

Yet what the spirit offers is often too august for our trivial minds. We accept the ease and relief and miss the inspirations of the day, where it comes from and what it stands for. This is why we pray for understanding:

May Thy children realize and understand that their rest comes from Thee, and that to rest means to sanctify Thy name.[12]

To observe the Sabbath is to celebrate the coronation of a day in the spiritual wonderland of time, the air of which we inhale when we "call it a delight."

Call the Sabbath a delight:[13] a delight to the soul and a delight to the body. Since there are so many acts which one must abstain from doing on the seventh day, "you might think I have given you the Sabbath for your displeasure; I have surely given you the Sabbath for your pleasure." To sanctify the seventh day does not mean: Thou shalt mortify thyself, but, on the contrary: Thou shalt sanctify it with all thy heart, with all thy soul and with all thy senses. "Sanctify the Sabbath by choice meals, by beautiful garments; delight your soul with pleasure and I will reward you for this very pleasure." [14]

Unlike the Day of Atonement, the Sabbath is not dedicated exclusively to spiritual goals. It is a day of the soul as well as of the body; comfort and pleasure are an integral part of the Sabbath observance. Man in his entirety, all his faculties must share its blessing.

A prince was once sent into captivity and compelled to live anonymously among rude and illiterate people. Years passed by, and he languished with longing for his royal father, for his native land. One day a secret communication reached him in which his father promised to bring him back to the palace, urging him not to unlearn his princely manner. Great was the joy of the prince, and he was eager to celebrate the day. But no one is able to celebrate alone. So he invited the people to the local tavern and ordered ample food and drinks for all of them. It was a sumptuous feast, and they were all full of rejoicing; the people because of the drinks and the prince in anticipation of his return to the palace.[15]—The soul cannot celebrate alone, so the body must be invited to partake in the rejoicing of the Sabbath.

"The Sabbath is a reminder of the two worlds—this world and the world to come; it is an example of both worlds. For the Sabbath is joy, holiness, and rest; joy is part of this world; holiness and rest are something of the world to come." [16]

To observe the seventh day does not mean merely to obey or to conform to the strictness of a divine command. To observe is to celebrate the creation of the world and to create the seventh day all over again, the majesty of holiness in time, "a day of rest, a day of freedom," a day which is like "a lord and king of all other days," [17] a lord and king in the commonwealth of time.

How should we weigh the difference between the Sabbath and the other days of the week? When a day like Wednesday arrives, the hours are blank, and unless we lend significance to them, they remain without character. The hours of the seventh day are significant in themselves; their significance and beauty do not depend on any work, profit or progress we may achieve. They have the beauty of grandeur.

Beauty of grandeur, a crown of victory, a day of rest
     and holiness . . . a rest in love and generosity,
     a true and genuine rest, a rest that yields peace
     and serenity, tranquility and security, a perfect
     rest *with which Thou art pleased*.[18]

Time is like a wasteland. It has grandeur but no beauty. Its strange, frightful power is always feared but rarely cheered. Then we arrive at the seventh day, and the Sabbath is endowed with a felicity which enraptures the soul, which glides into our thoughts with a healing sympathy. It is a day on which hours do not oust one another. It is a day that can soothe all sadness away.

No one, even the unlearned, the crude man, can remain insensitive to its beauty. "Even the unlearned is in awe of the day." [19] It is virtually impossible, the ancient rabbis believed, to tell a lie on the sacred Sabbath day.

What does the word "Sabbath" mean? According to some it is the name of the Holy One.[20] Since the word *Shabbat* is a name of God, one should not mention it in unclean places, where words of Torah should not be spoken. Some people were careful not to take it in vain.[21]

The seventh day is like a palace in time with a kingdom for all. It is not a date but an atmosphere.

It is not a different state of consciousness but a different climate; it is as if the appearance of all things somehow changed. The primary awareness is one of our being *within* the Sabbath rather than of the Sabbath being within us. We may not know whether our understanding is correct, or whether our sentiments are noble, but the air of the day surrounds us like spring which spreads over the land without our aid or notice.

"How precious is the Feast of Booths! Dwelling in the Booth, even our body is surrounded by the sanctity of the Mitzvah," said once a rabbi to his friend. Whereupon the latter remarked: "The Sabbath Day is even more than that. On the Feast you may leave the Booth for a while, whereas the Sabbath surrounds you wherever you go."

The difference between the Sabbath and all other days is not to be noticed in the physical structure of things, in their spatial dimension. Things do not change on that day. There is only a difference in the dimension of time, in the relation of the universe to God. The Sabbath preceded creation and the Sabbath completed creation; it is all of the spirit that the world can bear.

It is a day that ennobles the soul and makes the body wise. A tale may illustrate this point.

Once a rabbi was immured by his persecutors in a cave, where not a ray of light could reach him, so that he knew not when it was day or when it was night. Nothing tormented him so much as the thought that he was now hindered from celebrating the Sabbath with song and prayer, as he had been wont to do from his youth. Beside this an almost unconquerable desire to smoke caused him much pain. He worried and reproached himself that he could not conquer this passion. All at once, he perceived that it suddenly vanished; a voice said within him: "Now it is Friday evening! for this was always the hour when my longing for that which is forbidden on the Sabbath regularly left me." Joyfully he rose up and with loud voice thanked God and blessed the Sabbath day. So it went on from week to week; his tormenting desire for tobacco regularly vanished at the incoming of each Sabbath.[22]

It is one of life's highest rewards, a source of strength and inspiration to endure tribulation, to live nobly. The work on weekdays and the rest on the seventh day are correlated. The Sabbath is the inspirer, the other days the inspired.

The words: "On the *seventh* day God *finished* His work" (Genesis 2:2), seem to be a puzzle. Is it not said: "He *rested* on the *seventh* day"? "In *six* days the Lord made heaven and earth" (Exodus 20:11)? We would surely expect the Bible to tell us that on the sixth day God finished His work. Obviously, the ancient rabbis concluded, there was an act of creation on the seventh day. Just as heaven and earth were created in six days, *menuha* was created on the Sabbath.

"After the six days of creation—what did the universe still lack? *Menuha*. Came the Sabbath, came *menuha*, and the universe was complete." [23]

Menuha which we usually render with "rest" means here much more than withdrawal from labor and exertion, more than freedom from toil, strain or activity of any kind. *Menuha* is not a negative concept but something real and intrinsically positive. This must have been the view of the ancient rabbis if they believed that it took a special act of creation to bring it into being, that the universe would be incomplete without it.

"What was created on the seventh day? *Tranquility, serenity, peace* and *repose*." [24]

To the biblical mind *menuha* is the same as happiness [25] and stillness, as peace and harmony. The word with which Job described the state after life he was longing for is derived from the same root as *menuha*. It is the state wherein man lies still, wherein the wicked cease from troubling and the weary are at rest.[26] It is the state in which there is no strife and no fighting, no fear and no distrust. The essence of good life is *menuha*. "The Lord is my shepherd, I shall not want, He maketh me to lie down in green pastures; He leadeth me beside the still waters" (the waters of *menuhot*).[27] In later times *menuha* became a synonym for the life in the world to come, for eternal life.[28]

Six evenings a week we pray: "Guard our going out and our coming in"; on the Sabbath evening we pray instead: "Embrace us with a tent of Thy peace." Upon returning home from synagogue we intone the song:

> Peace be to you,
> Angels of Peace [29]

The seventh day sings. An old allegory asserts: "When Adam saw the majesty of the Sabbath, its greatness and glory, and the joy it conferred upon all beings, he intoned a song of praise for the Sabbath day as if *to give thanks to the Sabbath day*. Then God said to him: Thou singest a song of praise to the Sabbath day, and singest none to Me, the God of the Sabbath?

Thereupon the Sabbath rose from its seat, and prostrated herself before God, saying: It is a good thing *to give thanks unto the Lord*. And the whole of creation added: And to sing praise unto Thy Name, O Most High." [30]

"Angels have six wings, one for each day of the week, with which they chant their song; but they remain silent on the Sabbath, for it is the Sabbath which then chants a hymn to God." [31] It is the Sabbath that inspires all the creatures to sing praise to the Lord. In the language of the Sabbath morning liturgy:

To God who rested from all action on the seventh day
        and ascended upon His throne of glory.
He vested the day of rest with beauty;
He called the Sabbath a delight.
This is the song and the praise of the seventh day,
        on which God rested from His work.
The seventh day itself is uttering praise.
A song of the Sabbath day:
"It is good to give thanks unto the Lord!"
Therefore, all the creatures of God bless Him.

The Sabbath teaches all beings whom to praise.

II

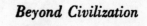

Beyond Civilization

Technical civilization is the product of labor, of man's exertion of power for the sake of gain, for the sake of producing goods. It begins when man, dissatisfied with what is available in nature, becomes engaged in a struggle with the forces of nature in order to enhance his safety and to increase his comfort. To use the language of the Bible, the task of civilization is to subdue the earth, to have dominion over the beast.

How proud we often are of our victories in the war with nature, proud of the multitude of instruments we have succeeded in inventing, of the abundance of commodities we have been able to produce. Yet our victories have come to resemble defeats. In spite of our triumphs, we have fallen victims to the work of our hands; it is as if the forces we had conquered have conquered us.

Is our civilization a way to disaster, as many of us are prone to believe? Is civilization essentially evil, to be rejected and condemned? The faith of the Jew is not a way out of this world, but a way of being within and above this world; not to reject but to surpass civilization. The Sabbath is the day on which we learn the art of *surpassing* civilization.

Adam was placed in the Garden of Eden "to dress it and to keep it" (Genesis 2:15). Labor is not only the destiny of man; it is endowed with divine dignity.

However, after he ate of the tree of knowledge he was condemned to toil, not only to labor "In toil shall thou eat . . . all the days of thy life" (Genesis 3:17). Labor is a blessing, toil is the misery of man.

The Sabbath as a day of abstaining from work is not a depreciation but an affirmation of labor, a divine exaltation of its dignity. Thou shalt abstain from labor on the seventh day is a sequel to the command: *Six days shalt thou labor, and do all thy work.*[1]

"Six days shalt thou labor and do all thy work; but the seventh day is Sabbath unto the Lord thy God." Just as we are commanded to keep the Sabbath, we are commanded to labor.[2] "Love work . . ."[3] The duty to work for six days is just as much a part of God's covenant with man as the duty to abstain from work on the seventh day.[4]

To set apart one day a week for freedom, a day on which we would not use the instruments which have been so easily turned into weapons of destruction, a day for being with ourselves, a day of detachment from the vulgar, of independence of external obligations, a day on which we stop worshipping the idols of technical civilization, a day on which we use no money, a day of armistice in the economic struggle with our fellow men and the forces of nature—is there any institution that holds out a greater hope for man's progress than the Sabbath?

The solution of mankind's most vexing problem will not be found in renouncing technical civilization, but in attaining some degree of independence of it.

In regard to external gifts, to outward possessions, there is only one proper attitude—to have them and to be able to do without them. On the Sabbath we live, as it were, *independent of technical civilization:* we abstain primarily from any activity that aims at remaking or reshaping the things of space. Man's royal privilege to conquer nature is suspended on the seventh day.

What are the kinds of labor not to be done on the Sabbath? They are, according to the ancient rabbis, all those acts which were necessary for the construction and furnishing of the Sanctuary in the desert.[5] The Sabbath itself is a sanctuary which we build, *a sanctuary in time.*

It is one thing to race or be driven by the vicissitudes that menace life, and another thing to stand still and to embrace the presence of an eternal moment.

The seventh day is the armistice in man's cruel struggle for existence, a truce in all conflicts, personal and social, peace between man and man, man and nature, peace within man; a day on which handling money is considered a desecration, on which man avows his independence of that which is the world's chief idol. The seventh day is the exodus from tension, the liberation of man from his own muddiness, the installation of man as a sovereign in the world of time.

In the tempestuous ocean of time and toil there are islands of stillness where man may enter a harbor and reclaim his dignity. The island is the seventh day, the Sabbath, a day of detachment from things, instruments and practical affairs as well as of attachment to the spirit.

The Sabbath must all be spent "in charm, grace, peace, and great love . . . for on it even the wicked in hell find peace." It is, therefore, a double sin to show anger on the Sabbath. "Ye shall kindle no fire throughout your habitations on the Sabbath day" (Exodus 35:3), is interpreted to mean: "Ye shall kindle no fire of controversy nor the heat of anger." [6] Ye shall kindle no fire—not even the fire of righteous indignation.

Out of the days through which we fight and from

whose ugliness we ache, we look to the Sabbath as our homeland, as our source and destination. It is a day in which we abandon our plebeian pursuits and reclaim our authentic state, in which we may partake of a blessedness in which we are what we are, regardless of whether we are learned or not, of whether our career is a success or a failure; it is a day of independence of social conditions.

All week we may ponder and worry whether we are rich or poor, whether we succeed or fail in our occupations; whether we accomplish or fall short of reaching our goals. But who could feel distressed when gazing at spectral glimpses of eternity, except to feel startled at the vanity of being so distressed?

The Sabbath is no time for personal anxiety or care, for any activity that might dampen the spirit of joy. The Sabbath is no time to remember sins, to confess, to repent or even to pray for relief or anything we might need. It is a day for praise, not a day for petitions. Fasting, mourning, demonstrations of grief are forbidden. The period of mourning is interrupted by the Sabbath. And if one visits the sick on the Sabbath, one should say: "It is the Sabbath, one must not complain; you will soon be cured." [7] One must abstain from toil and strain on the seventh day, even from strain in the service of God.[8]

Why are the Eighteen Benedictions not recited on the Sabbath? It is because the Sabbath was given to us by God for joy, for delight, for rest, and should not be marred by worry or grief. Should there be a sick one in the household, we might remember this while reciting the benediction: "Heal the sick," and would become saddened and gloomy on the Sabbath day. It is for this same reason that we recite in the Sabbath grace after meals the request that "there be no sadness or

trouble in the day of our rest." [9] It is a sin to be sad on
the Sabbath day.[10]

For the Sabbath is a day of harmony and peace,
peace between man and man, peace within man, and
peace with all things. On the seventh day man has no
right to tamper with God's world, to change the state of
physical things. It is a day of rest for *man and animal*
alike:

> In it thou shalt not do any manner of work, thou nor
> thy son, nor thy daughter, nor thy man-servant,
> nor thy maid-servant, nor thine *ox*, nor thine *ass*,
> nor any of thy *cattle*, nor thy stranger that is
> within thy gates; that thy man-servant and thy
> maid-servant may rest as well as thou.[11]

Rabbi Solomon of Radomsk once arrived in a certain town, where, he was told, lived an old woman who
had known the famous Rabbi Elimelech. She was too
old to go out, so he went to see her and asked her to
tell him what she knew about the great Master.

—I do not know what went on in his room, because I
worked as one of the maids in the kitchen of his house.
Only one thing I can tell you. During the week the
maids would often quarrel with one another, as is common. But, week after week, on Friday when the Sabbath was about to arrive, the spirit in the kitchen was
like the spirit on the eve of the Day of Atonement.
Everybody would be overcome with an urge to ask for-
giveness of each other. We were all seized by a feeling
of affection and inner peace.[12]

The Sabbath, thus, is more than an armistice, more
than an interlude; it is a profound conscious harmony
of man and the world, a sympathy for all things and a
participation in the spirit that unites what is below and

what is above. All that is divine in the world is brought into union with God. This is Sabbath, and the true happiness of the universe.

"Six days shalt thou labor and do all thy work (Exodus 20:8). Is it possible for a human being to do all his work in six days? Does not our work always remain incomplete? What the verse means to convey is: Rest on the Sabbath as if all your work were done. Another interpretation: *Rest even from the thought of labor*." [13]

A pious man once took a stroll in his vineyard on the Sabbath. He saw a breach in the fence, and then determined to mend it when the Sabbath would be over. At the expiration of the Sabbath he decided: since the thought of repairing the fence occurred to me on the Sabbath I shall never repair it. [14]

Part Two
III

The Splendor of Space

An allegorical interpretation of an ancient debate.

The time: about the year 130.

The place: Palestine.

The people present: Three leading scholars and one outsider. The place and the people under the dominion of the Roman Empire.

Rabbi Judah ben Ilai, Rabbi Jose, and Rabbi Shimeon ben Yohai were sitting together, and with them was a man called Judah ben Gerim. Rabbi Judah opened the discussion and said:

—How fine are the works of this people (the Romans)! They have made roads and market places, they have built bridges, they have erected bathhouses.

Rabbi Jose was silent.

Then Rabbi Shimeon ben Yohai replied and said:

—All that they made they made for themselves. They made roads and market places to put harlots there; they built bridges to levy tolls for them; they erected bathhouses to delight their bodies.

Judah ben Gerim went home and related to his father and mother all that had been said. And the report of it spread until it reached the government. Decreed the government:

—Judah who exalted us shall be exalted; Jose who was silent shall go into exile; Shimeon who reviled our work shall be put to death.

When Rabbi Shimeon heard of the decree, he took

his son Rabbi Eleazar with him and hid in the House of Learning. And his wife came every day and brought him stealthily bread and a jug of water. When Rabbi Shimeon heard that men were searching for them and trying to capture them, he said to his son:

—We cannot rely upon a woman's discretion, for she can easily be talked over. Or perhaps she may be tortured until she discloses our place of concealment.

So they went together into the field and hid themselves in a cave, so that no man knew what had become of them. And a miracle happened: a carob tree grew up inside the cave and a well of water opened, so that they had enough to eat and enough to drink. They took off their clothes and sat up to their necks in sand. The whole day they studied Torah. And when the time for prayer came, they put their clothes on and prayed, and then they put them off and again dug themselves into the sand, so that their clothes should not wear away. Thus they spent twelve years in the cave.

When the twelve years had come to an end, Elijah the prophet came and, standing at the entrance of the cave, exclaimed:

—Who will inform the son of Yohai that the emperor is dead and his decree has been annulled?

When they heard this, they emerged from the cave. Seeing the people plowing the fields and sowing the seed, they exclaimed:

—These people forsake eternal life and are engaged in temporary life!

Whatever they looked upon was immediately consumed by the fire of their eyes. Thereupon a voice from heaven exclaimed:

—Have ye emerged to destroy My world? Return to your cave!

So they returned and dwelled there another twelve

months; for, they said, the punishment of the wicked in hell lasts only twelve months.

When the twelve months had come to an end, the voice was heard from heaven saying:

—Go forth from your cave!

Thus they went out. Wherever Rabbi Eleazar hurt, Rabbi Shimeon healed. Said Rabbi Shimeon:

—My son, if only we two remain to study the Torah, that will be sufficient for the world.

It was the eve of the Sabbath when they left the cave, and as they came out they saw an old man carrying two bundles of myrtle in his hand, a sweet-smelling herb having the perfume of paradise.

—What are these for, they asked him.

—They are in honor of the Sabbath, the old man replied.

Said Rabbi Shimeon to his son:

—Behold and see how dear God's commands are to Israel . . .

At that moment they both found tranquility of soul.[1]

There is a mass of cryptic meaning in this silent, solitary story of one who, outraged by the scandal of desecrated time, refused to celebrate the splendor of civilized space. It symbolically describes how Rabbi Shimeon ben Yohai and his son went from exasperation and disgust with this world, which resulted in their actually trying to destroy those who were engaged in worldly activities, to a reconciliation with this world. What stirred these men was not, as it is usually understood by historians,[2] mere patriotic resentment against the power that had vanquished and persecuted the people of Judea. From the development of the story, it becomes obvious that from the outset the issue was not only the Roman rule but also the Roman civilization. After they had spent twelve years in the cave, the scope of the issue expanded even further. It was not any more a particular civilization but all civilization, the worth of worldly living that became the problem.

Rome, in that period, was at the height of her glory. She was the mistress of the world. All the Mediterranean countries lay at her feet. Her commerce extended beyond the bounds of the Empire to Scandinavia in the north and China in the east, and her civilization attained a high degree of perfection in the technical arts. In all her provinces, signs of immense progress in administration, engineering and the art of construction were widely visible. It was the ambition of her rulers to express the splendor of their age by adorning with public monuments every province of the empire. Fora, theaters, amphitheaters, public baths, aqueducts and bridges constructed in many cities were often marvels of constructive skill.

Rome herself towered in her glory as the city on which "the looks of men and gods were turned." Even generations after that period, a poet could still aver "that Heaven could show nothing fairer; that no eye could see her immensity, no heart feel her beauty, no tongue sing all her praise." [3] The Colosseum with its overwhelming massiveness, the Pantheon with its lofty vaulting, and particularly the Forum of Trajan, a building of unparalleled magnificence and "admired even by the gods," seemed to proclaim that the Empire and eternity were one. The ancient man was inclined to believe that monuments will last for ever. [4] It was, therefore, fit to bestow the most precious epithet on Rome and to call it: *the Eternal City*. [5] The state became an object of worship, a divinity; and the Emperor embodied its divinity as he embodied its sovereignty.

It was hard not to be impressed by the triumphs of

that great Empire and to disagree with the mild and
gentle Rabbi Judah ben Ilai who acknowledged the
boon it had brought to many lands: "How fine are the
works of this people! They have made streets, they
have built bridges, they have erected baths!" And yet,
to Rabbi Shimeon ben Yohai these triumphs were
shocking, hateful and repulsive. He disparaged the
calculating, utilitarian spirit of Roman civilization. He
knew that all these splendid edifices and public insti-
tutions were not built by the Romans to aid the people
but to serve their own nefarious designs: "All that they
made they made for themselves." [6]

When Rabbi Shimeon ben Yohai abandoned the
world of civilization to spend many years in a cave,
sitting up to his neck in sand, he forfeited worldly life
to attain "eternal life." Yet this was an attainment
which was hardly meaningful to his persecutors. To
most Romans eternity was almost a worldly concept.
The survival of the soul consisted not in being carried
away to a superterrestrial and blessed existence. Immortality meant either fame or the cleaving to one's
home, to one's earthly abode even after death. But
Rabbi Shimeon abandoned home as well as the road to
fame which is usually attained by one's being active in
the affairs of the world. He fled from the world where
eternity was the attribute of a city and went to the cave
where he found a way to endow life with a quality of
eternity.

The Romans had no conviction that there was any
after-life at all, certainly no conviction of an immortal felicity or retribution.[7] The ardent longing for such
a belief was something which the Roman spirit could
not satisfy. "The body dies, the personality disap-
pears, nothing remains alive except the remembrance
of virtue and accomplishments of the deceased." [8] The
term immortality became *a metaphor,* signifying one's

being remembered by the people; a metaphor which to this day holds many preachers in its spell. In an appeal to the Senate that to the soldiers of the Martian legion who had fallen in battle "there be raised a monument in the noblest possible shape," Cicero said: "Brief is the life given us by nature; but the memory of life nobly resigned is everlasting . . . There shall therefore be erected a mass of splendid workmanship and an inscription cut; and—apostrophizing the fallen soldiers—in your praise, whether men shall behold your monument or shall hear of it, never shall the language of deepest gratitude be silent. Thus, in exchange for life's mortal state, you will have gained for yourself immortality." [9] He spoke at another occasion of a public meeting at which "the entire people of Rome accorded to me, not a vote of thanks which would pass with the day, but eternity and immortality." [10] Indeed, it was precisely the understanding of what eternity means that determined Rabbi Shimeon's withdrawal from the world. It was the kind of an idea that would occasionally emerge in the minds of Stoic philosophers in Rome and that inspired Seneca to say that the gods order us "to prepare ourselves to join them at some future time and to plan for immortality." [10a]

The rewards that most people woo were of little worth to Rabbi Shimeon ben Yohai. He was not captivated by the things of the earth, by all the world that is bound to decay. Or was the fame one attained among men to be considered eternal? What is the worth of being remembered by men?

All flesh is grass, all the goodliness thereof is as the
    flower of the field . . .
The grass withereth, the flower fadeth; but the word
    of our God shall stand forever.[11]

The world is transitory, but that by which the world was created—the word of God—is everlasting.[12] Eternity is attained by dedicating one's life to the word of God, to the study of Torah.

To this day, the idea of Torah being the source of eternity is proclaimed in our prayers. It is for the gift of perceiving the taste of eternity in dedication to the Torah that time and again we thank and say: "Blessed be thou . . . who has given us the Torah . . . and has planted within us *eternal life*." [13] And when we go hence and rest in the world to come—what is the bliss that awaits the souls of righteous men? It is to begin to understand the deeper meaning of the Torah: "Things that are covered up from men in this world will become transparent as globes of crystal." [14]

To Rabbi Shimeon eternity was not attained by those who bartered time for space but by those who knew how to fill their time with spirit. To him the great problem was *time* rather than *space*; the task was how to convert time into eternity rather than how to fill space with buildings, bridges and roads; and the solution of the problem lay in study and prayer rather than in geometry and engineering.

IV

Only Heaven and Nothing Else?

It was not the force of despair that bred Rabbi Shimeon's contempt for the affairs of this world. Behind his blunt repudiation of worldliness we discern a thirst for the treasures of eternity and a sense of horror at seeing how people were wasting their lives in the pursuit *of temporary life,* and neglecting the pursuit of *eternal life.* In his boundless thirst, he saw no middle way, no ground for compromise. The duty to study Torah—which was the way to attain eternity—had an exclusive claim on all of life: *"This book of the Torah shall not depart out of thy mouth but thou shalt meditate therein day and night"* (Joshua 1:8). To abate, to relent even for an hour was to forfeit a part of eternal life, an act of partial suicide. Hence Rabbi Shimeon could not but regard any secular activity as iniquity.

An older contemporary of Rabbi Shimeon ben Yohai, the distinguished heretic Alisha ben Abuyah, had taken the opposite view. Charmed with the worldly culture of Hellenism, he would visit the schools and attempt to entice the students from the study of the Torah and urge them to dedicate their energies to some more practical occupation:

"Out with you, you lazy people, stop idling away your days. Begin a human work: you become a carpenter, and you a mason, you a tailor, and you a fisherman." [1]

Rabbi Shimeon's renunciation of this world and Elisha's infatuation with this world represented an extremism which found little acclamation among their contemporaries. The saintly Rabbi Judah ben Ilai, who argued with Rabbi Shimeon in favor of the Romans, rejected Rabbi Shimeon's immoderate demands of man. Personally, Rabbi Judah was given to severe self-denial and austerity. "I do not wish to derive any pleasure from this world," [2] he said. Yet his advice to others was that the ideal path lay midway. Life is likened unto two roads: one of fire and one of ice. "If you walk in the one, you will be burned, and if in the other, you will be frozen. What shall one do? Walk in the middle." [3]

Quite different was the outlook of Rabbi Shimeon. "Scripture says: *And thou shalt gather in thy corn* (Deuteronomy 11:14)—what has this teaching to tell us? Since it is written: *This book of the Torah shall not depart out of thy mouth but thou shalt meditate therein day and night* (Joshua 1:8), it is possible to think that these words are to be understood as they are written (namely, that no time be devoted to any other activity, such as earning a livelihood); therefore there is a teaching to say: *And thou shalt gather in thy corn*, i.e., conduct at the same time a worldly occupation. These are the words of Rabbi Ishmael. Rabbi Shimeon ben Yohai says: Is it possible for a man to plow at the time of plowing, sow at the time of sowing, harvest at the time of harvesting, thresh at the time of threshing, and winnow at the time of winnowing—what is to become of Torah?" [4]

Rabbi Shimeon and his son appear in this story as the antipodes of Prometheus. When Zeus, in an act of revenge, withheld fire from men, Prometheus stole it from the deity in heaven and brought it down to men on earth, concealed in a hollow stalk, and taught them the use of the technical arts. For this he was honored by men as the founder of civilization, and for this he was punished by the gods and was chained to a rock where every day an eagle ate his liver, which was healed again at night.[5] In contrast, Rabbi Shimeon tried, as it were, to take away fire from men, reproving them for pursuing the art of cultivating the ground. For this he was remonstrated by a heavenly voice and punished by being placed in confinement in a cave for twelve months.

The most baffling moment of the story comes at the end, in the epilogue. After spending twelve years in the cave in study and prayer, the two saints persisted in their condemnation of all worldly activities. Having been reproved by a heavenly voice, and having spent twelve more penitential months in the cave, the father was cured of his world-negation. The son, however, did not make peace with the world even then; not until both encountered the sight of "the old man" holding two bundles of myrtle in honor of the Sabbath, and that sight gave both of them tranquility of spirit. What was the symbolic significance of that sight? Why did it indicate a solution to the tragic problem of civilization?

Rabbi Shimeon's doctrine was: There is only heaven and nothing else; but heaven contradicted him and said: There is heaven and everything else. His martial anger was sharply broken by the Voice: *Have ye emerged to destroy my World?* What Rabbi Shimeon decried, the Voice endorsed.

It was not until Rabbi Shimeon and his son came out of the cave at the end of their second period of retreat that their minds were reconciled to the idea that the world this side of heaven is worth working in. What caused the change of mind?

It was the "old man"—symbolizing the people of Israel—who went out to meet the Sabbath with myrtles in his hand as if the Sabbath were *a bride*.

The myrtle was, in ancient times, the symbol of love, the plant of the bride. When going out to invite his friends to the wedding, the groom would carry myrtle sprigs in his hands.[6] At the wedding ceremony it was customary in some places to recite the blessing over the myrtle.[7] An overhead awning of myrtle was erected for the bride,[8] while the groom wore a garland of roses or myrtles.[9] It was customary to perform a dance with myrtle branches before the bride. Rabbi Judah ben Ilai, the colleague of Rabbi Shimeon ben Yohai, known to us from his part in the debate about Rome, was praised for his efforts in bringing joy to every bride. He would take myrtle twigs to a wedding, dance before the bride and exclaim: Beautiful and graceful bride! [10] The "old man" who was running at twilight to welcome the Sabbath, holding two bundles of myrtle in his hands,[11] personified the idea of Israel welcoming the Sabbath as a bride.[12]

To the Romans technical civilization was the highest goal, and time for the sake of space. To Rabbi Shimeon spiritual life was the highest goal, and time for the sake of eternity. His conclusive comfort was: in spite of all dedication to temporal things, there was a destiny that would save the people of Israel, a commitment deeper than all interests—the commitment to the Sabbath.

This, then, is the answer to the problem of civilization: not to flee from the realm of space; to work with things of space but to be in love with eternity. Things are our tools; eternity, the Sabbath, is our mate. Israel is engaged to eternity. Even if they dedicate six days of the week to worldly pursuits, their soul is claimed by the seventh day.

V

"Thou Art One"

An allegory.

At the beginning time was one, eternal. But time undivided, time eternal, would be unrelated to the world of space. So time was divided into seven days and entered into an intimate relationship with the world of space. With every single day, another realm of things came into being, except on the seventh day. The Sabbath was a lonely day. It may be compared to a king who has seven sons. To six of them he gave his wealth, and the youngest one he endowed with nobility, with the prerogative of royalty. The six older sons who were commoners found their mates, but the noble one remained without a mate.

Says Rabbi Shimeon ben Yohai:

After the work of creation was completed, the Seventh Day pleaded: Master of the universe, all that Thou hast created is in couples; to every day of the week Thou gavest a mate; only I was left alone. And God answered: The Community of Israel will be your *mate*.

That promise was not forgotten. "When the people of Israel stood before the mountain of Sinai, the Lord said to them: 'Remember that I said to the Sabbath: The Community of Israel is your mate.' Hence: *Remember* the Sabbath day to sanctify it" (Exodus 20:8). The Hebrew word *le-kadesh*, to sanctify, means, in the language of the Talmud, to consecrate a woman, to betroth. Thus the meaning of that word on Sinai was to impress upon Israel the fact that their destiny is to be the groom of the sacred day, the commandment to espouse the seventh day.[1]

With all its grandeur, the Sabbath is not sufficient unto itself. Its spiritual reality calls for companionship of man. There is a great longing in the world. The six days stand in need of space; the seventh day stands in need of man. It is not good that the spirit should be alone, so Israel was destined to be a helpmeet for the Sabbath.

To understand the significance of that new conception, it is important to be aware of the mood of the age. Rabbi Shimeon belonged to a generation which, under the leadership of Bar Kochba, rose in arms against the might of Rome in a last effort to regain independence and to rebuild the Temple in Jerusalem. Israel without the sanctuary seemed alone in the world. The revolt was crushed; it became clear that there was no possibility of another uprising. The sanctuary in space was going to remain in ruins for many a long day. But Rabbi Shimeon's idea proclaimed Israel was not alone. Israel is engaged to holiness, to eternity. The match was made long before history began; the Sabbath was a union that no one could disjoin. What God put together could not be set apart.

At a time when, in Rome, the deification of the Emperor was an official doctrine, Rabbi Shimeon extolled the most abstract of things: time, the seventh day. Jewish tradition had an aversion to personification, yet in their allegories it rhetorically personified the wisdom of the Torah. The boldness of Rabbi Shimeon was in extolling a day and in proclaiming the intimate union of Israel and the Sabbath.

Rabbi Shimeon's concept alludes to the idea that

man's relation to the spirit is not one-sided; there is a
reciprocity between man and the spirit. The Sabbath is
not only a legal institution, a state of mind or a form
of conduct, but a process in the world of spirit. At the
beginning of time there was a longing, the longing of
the Sabbath for man.

Through Rabbi Shimeon ben Yohai, the light of a
great idea was caught in the mirror of a word, one that
conveys the destiny of a people and the nimbus of a
day. It did not remain a theory; it was an insight that
made history. Ingrained in the soul of the people, it
found expression throughout the ages in their thoughts,
songs and customs.

Only two generations had gone by since the time of
Rabbi Shimeon and there was a new tone in the celebration of the day. About the middle of the third century, distinguished scholars speak of the seventh day
not as if referring to abstract time, elusive and constantly passing us by. The day was a living presence,
and when it arrived they felt as if a guest had come to
see them. And, surely, a guest who comes to pay a call
in friendship or respect must be given a welcome. It is,
indeed, told of Rabbi Yannai that his custom was to
don his robes on the eve of the Sabbath, and then ad-
dress himself to the ethereal guest: *"Come O Bride,
Come O Bride."* [2] Of another contemporary, Rabbi
Hanina the Great, we know that at the sunset of Sabbath eve, he would clothe himself in beautiful robes,
burst forth in a dance[3] and exclaim, presumably in the
presence of his friends: "Come, let us go out to welcome the *Queen Sabbath.*" [4]

There are two aspects to the Sabbath, as there are
two aspects to the world. The Sabbath is meaningful
to man and is meaningful to God. It stands in a relation to both, and is a sign of the covenant entered into

by both. What is the sign? God has sanctified the day, and man must again and again sanctify the day, illumine the day with the light of his soul. The Sabbath is holy by the grace of God, and is still in need of all the holiness which man may lend to it.

The Sabbath is meaningful to God, for without it there would be no holiness in our world of time. In discussing the meaning of the verse, "and on the *seventh* day He finished His work," [5] the ancient rabbis suggested that an act of creation took place on the seventh day. The world would not be complete if the six days did not culminate in the Sabbath. Geniba and the rabbis discussed this.[6] Geniba said: This may be compared to a king who made a bridal chamber, which he plastered, painted and adorned; now what did the bridal chamber lack? A bride to enter it. Similarly, what did the universe still lack? The Sabbath. The rabbis said: Imagine a king who made a ring: What did it lack? A signet. Similarly, what did the universe lack? The Sabbath.[7]

The Sabbath is a bride, and its celebration is like a wedding.

"We learn in the Midrash that the Sabbath is like unto a bride. Just as a bride when she comes to her groom is lovely, bedecked and perfumed, so the Sabbath comes to Israel lovely and perfumed, as it is written: *And on the Seventh Day He ceased from work and He rested* (Exodus 31:17), and immediately afterwards we read: *And He gave unto Moses kekalloto* [the word *kekalloto* means when he finished, but it may also mean] as his bride,[8] to teach us that just as a bride is lovely and bedecked, so is the Sabbath lovely and bedecked; just as a groom is dressed in his finest garments, so is a man on the Sabbath day dressed in his finest garments; just as a man rejoices all the days of the wedding feast, so does man rejoice on the Sabbath; just as the groom does no work on his wedding day, so does a man abstain from work on the Sabbath day; and therefore the Sages and ancient Saints called the Sabbath a bride.

"There is a hint of this in the Sabbath prayers. In the Friday evening service we say *Thou hast sanctified the seventh day*, referring to the marriage of the bride to the groom (sanctification is the Hebrew word for marriage). In the morning prayer we say: *Moses rejoiced in the gift* [of the Sabbath] bestowed upon him which corresponds to the groom's rejoicing with the bride. In the additional prayer we make mention of *the two lambs, the fine flour for a meal offering, mingled with oil and the drink thereof* referring to the meat, the bread, the wine, and the oil used in the wedding banquet. [In the last hour of the day we say] *Thou art One* to parallel the consummation of the marriage by which the bride and groom are united." [9]

VI

The Presence of a Day

●

What is it that these epithets are trying to celebrate? It is time, of all phenomena the least tangible, the least material. When we celebrate the Sabbath we adore precisely something we do not see. To name it queen, to call it bride is merely to allude to the fact that its spirit is a reality we meet rather than an empty span of time which we choose to set aside for comfort or recuperation.

Did the rabbis imagine that the Sabbath was an angel? a spiritual person? [1] Religious thought cannot afford to associate closely with the powers of fantasy. Yet the metaphoric concept of the Sabbath held no danger of deification of the seventh day, of conceiving it to be an angel or a spiritual person. Nothing stands between God and man, not even a day.

The idea of the Sabbath as a queen or a bride did not represent a mental image, something that could be imagined. There was no picture in the mind that corresponded to the metaphor. Nor was it ever cystallized as a definite concept, from which logical consequences could be drawn, or raised to a dogma, an object of belief. The same Rabbi Hanina who celebrated the Sabbath as a queen preferred on another occasion to compare the Sabbath with a king. [2]

It would be an oversimplification to assume that the ancient rabbis were trying to personify the Sabbath, to express an image which was in their minds. Between personifying time and calling it queen or bride the difference is as big as between presuming to count the exact sum of all beings and calling it universe. The rabbis did not believe that the seventh day was endowed with human features, with a figure or a face; their ideas did not result in either visible or verbal iconography. They rarely went beyond the venture of cherishing the endearing terms of queen or bride. This was not because of a dearth in imaginative power but because what they were eager to convey was more than what minds could visualize or words could say.

To most of us a person, a human being, seems to be a maximum of being, the ceiling of reality; we think that to personify is to glorify. Yet do not some of us realize at times that a person is no superlative, that to personify the spiritually real is to belittle it? A personification may be both a distortion and a depreciation. There are many persons in the world but only one Sabbath.

The idea of the Sabbath as a queen or a bride is not a personification of the Sabbath but an exemplification of a divine attribute, an illustration of God's need for human love; it does not represent a substance but the presence of God, His relationship to man.

Such metaphorical exemplification does not state a fact; it expresses a value, putting into words the preciousness of the Sabbath as Sabbath. Observance of the seventh day is more than a technique of fulfilling a commandment. The Sabbath is the presence of God in the world, open to the soul of man. It is possible for the soul to respond in affection, to enter into fellowship with the consecrated day.

The seventh day was full of both loveliness and majesty—an object of awe, attention and love. Friday eve, when the Sabbath is about to engross the world, the mind, the entire soul, and the tongue is tied with trembling and joy—what is there that one could say? To those who are not vulgarized, who guard their words from being tainted, queen, bride, signify majesty tempered with mercy and delicate innocence that is waiting for affection.

The idea of the Sabbath as a bride was retained by Israel; it is the theme of the hymn *Lechah Dodi* chanted in the synagogue. Even the sanctification over wine was explained with the idea that, just as the wedding ceremony is performed over a cup of wine, so Sabbath is "the bride that enters the *hupah*." To this day the meal on Saturday night is called *"the escort of the queen."*

"The reason why the people extend the observance of the Sabbath to a part of Saturday night is to thank and to show that they do not like to see the departure of the holy guest, that her parting evokes a deep feeling of regret. This is why they detain her, and in their great affection accompany her with song and praise . . . as it is said in a Midrash: This may be compared to a bride and queen who is escorted with song and praise." [3]

The name of the Friday evening service is *kabbalat Shabbat*. What does the phrase mean? The term *kabbalah* denotes the act of taking an obligation upon oneself. The term in this sense has the connotation of strictness and restraint. Yet *kabbalah* in its verbal form means also: to receive, to welcome, to greet.[4] In the first meaning, it is applied to a law; in the second, to a person. The question arises, in what meaning is the word *kabbalah* used when applied to the word *Shabbat?*

It has been said that in medieval literature the term

kabbalat Shabbat is used exclusively in the first sense, denoting the act of taking upon oneself the obligation to rest,[5] the moment of cessation from work. Yet it may be proved that in an even earlier period the term has been used in the sense of greeting or welcoming the Sabbath.[6] What, then, does the phrase *kabbalat Shabbat* mean?

The answer is, it means both; it has both a legal and a spiritual meaning; they are inseparable from one another. The distinction of the Sabbath is reflected in the twin meanings of the phrase *kabbalat Shabbat* which means to accept the sovereignty as well as to welcome the presence of the day. The Sabbath is a queen as well as a bride.

Part Three

VII

Eternity Utters a Day

Six days a week the spirit is alone, disregarded, for·
saken, forgotten. Working under strain, beset with
worries, enmeshed in anxieties, man has no mind for
ethereal beauty. But the spirit is waiting for man to
join it.

Then comes the sixth day. Anxiety and tension give
place to the excitement that precedes a great event. The
Sabbath is still away but the thought of its imminent
arrival stirs in the heart a passionate eagerness to be
ready and worthy to receive it.

"It is incumbent on every man to be very, very zeal-
ous in making the Sabbath day preparations, to be
prompt and diligent as a man who has heard that the
queen is coming to lodge at his house, or that the bride
and her entire entourage are coming to his home. What
would such a man do? He would rejoice greatly and
exclaim: 'What a great honor they do me by their
coming to dwell under my roof!' He would say to
his servants: 'Arrange the house, clean and tidy it, and
prepare the beds in honor of the arrival, and I will go
to purchase the bread, meat and fish—whatever I can
obtain in their honor.' Such a man will busy himself
in the preparation of the Sabbath food, even though he
have a thousand servants.

"Now who is greater than the Sabbath which is both
bride and queen and who is called delightful. A thou-

sand times more so should the master of the house himself be busy in making the preparations, even though he may have a hundred servants." [1]

"This was the practice of Rabbi Judah ben Ilai—on the eve of the Sabbath a basin filled with hot water was brought to him, and he washed his face, hands and feet, and he wrapped himself and sat in fringed linen robes, and was like an angel of the Lord of hosts." [2]

"When Rabbi Hamnuna the Ancient used to come out from the river on a Friday afternoon (after taking his bath), he was wont to rest a little on the bank, and, raising his eyes in gladness, he would say that he sat there in order to behold the joyous sight of the heavenly angels ascending and descending. At each arrival of the Sabbath, he said, man is caught up into the world of souls. Happy is he who is aware of the mysteries of his Lord." [3]

When all work is brought to a standstill, the candles are lit. Just as creation began with the word, "Let there be light!" so does the celebration of creation begin with the kindling of lights. It is the woman who ushers in the joy and sets up the most exquisite symbol, light, to dominate the atmosphere of the home.

And the world becomes a place of rest. An hour arrives like a guide, and raises our minds above accustomed thoughts. People assemble to welcome the wonder of the seventh day, while the Sabbath sends out its presence over the fields, into our homes, into our hearts. It is a moment of resurrection of the dormant spirit in our souls.

Refreshed and renewed, attired in festive garments, with candles nodding dreamily to unutterable expectations, to intuitions of eternity, some of us are overcome with a feeling, as if almost all they would say

would be like a veil. There is not enough grandeur in
our souls to be able to unravel in words the knot of
time and eternity. One should like to sing for all men,
for all generations. Some people chant the greatest of
all songs: *The Song of Songs.* What ancient attachment, what an accumulation of soul is flowing in their
chant! It is a chant of love for God, a song of passion,
nostalgia and tender apology.

Set me as a seal upon thy heart,
As a seal upon thy arm;
For love is strong as death,
Jealousy is cruel as the grave:
The coals thereof are coals of fire,
A most vehement flame.
Many waters cannot quench love,
Neither can the floods drown it;
If a man would give all the substance of his house for
    love,
He would utterly be contemned.

A thought has blown the market place away. There
is a song in the wind and joy in the trees. The Sabbath
arrives in the world, scattering a song in the silence of
the night: eternity utters a day. Where are the words
that could compete with such might?

The voice of the Lord is upon the waters . . .
The voice of the Lord is powerful;
The voice of the Lord is full of majesty . . .
And strippeth the forests bare:
And in His temple all say: Glory.

We all go out to welcome the queen, to serenade the
bride.

Come, Beloved, meet the Bride!
Let us go and welcome the Sabbath!

Zion is in ruins, Jerusalem lies in the dust. All week there is only hope of redemption. But when the Sabbath is entering the world, man is touched by a moment of actual redemption; as if for a moment the spirit of the Messiah moved over the face of the earth.

Shrine of the King, royal city, arise!
Come forth from thy ruins.
Long enough have you dwelt in the vale of tears . . .
Shake off your dust, arise!
Put on your glorious garments, my people . . .
Be not ashamed nor confounded.
Why are you downcast?
Why do you moan?
The afflicted of my people will be sheltered within you;
The city shall be rebuilt on its ancient site . . .
Your God will rejoice over you
As a bridegroom rejoices over his bride.

Before the last stanza the congregation rises and turns to the west as a sign of welcoming the invisible guest. They all bow their heads in greeting.

Come in peace, crown of God,
Come with joy and cheerfulness,
Amidst the faithful, precious people . . .
Come, Beloved, meet the Bride.

The Sabbath comes like a caress, wiping away fear, sorrow and somber memories. It is already night when joy begins, when a beautifying surplus of soul visits our mortal bones and lingers on.

We do not know how to thank and to say:

With wisdom Thou openest the gates of heaven . . .
Thou changest times . . .
Thou rollest away darkness before light . . .
Thou makest the distinction between day and night.

But there is something greater than the marvel of
the world: the spirit. In His world we sense His wisdom, in His spirit we see His love.

With eternal love Thou hast loved the house of Israel
    Torah, mitzvot, laws and judgements Thou hast
    taught us.
    Mayest Thou never take away Thy love from us.

Then we hear again the words of Moses urging us
to learn how to reciprocate the divine love.

Thou shalt love The Lord, Thy God
With all thy heart, with all thy soul,
And with all thy might . . .

Then we read the words of God:

Remember to do all the commands of the Lord, and
    ye will not follow the desires of your heart and
    your eyes that lead you astray.
I am the Lord your God, who brought you out of the
    land of Egypt to be your God; I am the Lord
    your God.

And this is the response:

True and certain is all this,
He is the Lord our God, no one else, and we Israel are
    His people.

If we only had enough spirit to comprehend His sovereignty, to live in His kingdom. But our mind is weak, divided our spirit.

Spread Thou over us Thy shelter of peace,
Direct us aright with Thine good counsel . . .
Save us for Thy name's sake.

VIII

Intuitions of Eternity

That the Sabbath and eternity are one—or of the same essence—is an ancient idea.[1] A legend relates that "at the time when God was giving the Torah to Israel, He said to them: My children! If you accept the Torah and observe my mitzvot, I will give you for all eternity a thing most precious that I have in my possession.

—And what, asked Israel, is that precious thing which Thou wilt give us if we obey Thy Torah?

—The world to come.

—Show us in this world an example of the world to come.

—The Sabbath is an example of the world to come." [2]

An ancient tradition declares: "The world to come is characterized by the kind of holiness possessed by the Sabbath in this world . . . The Sabbath possesses a holiness like that of the world to come." [3]

Rabbi Akiba, the teacher of Rabbi Shimeon ben Yohai, gave expression to the same idea. "There was a special song for every day of the week which the Levites used to sing in the Temple at Jerusalem. On the first day they sang *The Earth is the Lord's*; on the second day they sang *Great is the Lord*, and so on. On the Sabbath they sang *A Psalm: a Song for the Sabbath Day*; a Psalm, a song for the time that is to come, for the day which will be all Sabbath and rest in the life eternal." [4]

What is the nature of the day that is all Sabbath? It is a time in which "there is neither eating nor drinking nor worldly transactions; but the righteous sit enthroned, their crowns on their heads, and enjoy the luster of the Shechinah." [5]

According to the Talmud, the Sabbath is *me'en 'olam ha-ba*, which means: *somewhat like* eternity or the world to come. This idea that a seventh part of our lives may be experienced as paradise is a scandal to the pagans and a revelation to the Jews. And yet to Rabbi Hayim of Krasne the Sabbath contains more than a morsel of eternity. To him the Sabbath is the fountainhead (*ma'yan*) of eternity, the well from which heaven or the life in the world to come takes its source.

Unless one learns how to relish the taste of Sabbath while still in this world, unless one is initiated in the appreciation of eternal life, one will be unable to enjoy the taste of eternity in the world to come. Sad is the lot of him who arrives inexperienced and when led to heaven has no power to perceive the beauty of the Sabbath. . . . [6]

While Jewish tradition offers us no definition of the concept of eternity, it tells us how to experience the taste of eternity or eternal life within time. Eternal life does not grow away from us; it is "planted within us," [7] growing beyond us. The world to come is therefore not only a posthumous condition, dawning upon the soul on the morrow after its departure from the body. The essence of the world to come is Sabbath eternal, and the seventh day in time is an example of eternity. [8] The seventh day has the flavor of the seventh heaven and was given as a foretaste of the world to come; *ot hi le-'olam,* a token of eternity. [9]

A story is told about a rabbi who once entered heaven in his dream. He was permitted to approach the temple in Paradise where the great sages of the Talmud, the Tannaim, were spending their eternal lives. He saw that they were just sitting around tables studying the Talmud. The disappointed rabbi wondered, "Is this all there is to Paradise?" But suddenly he heard a voice: "You are mistaken. The Tannaim are not in Paradise. Paradise is in the Tannaim."

There is much that philosophy could learn from the Bible. To the philosopher the idea of the good is the most exalted idea. But to the Bible the idea of the good is penultimate; it cannot exist without the holy. The good is the base, the holy is the summit. Things created in six days He considered *good*, the seventh day He made *holy*.

To Jewish piety the ultimate human dichotomy is not that of mind and matter but that of the sacred and the profane. We have known profanity too long and have become accustomed to think that the soul is an automaton. The law of the Sabbath tries to direct the body and the mind to the dimension of the holy. It tries to teach us that man stands not only in a relation to nature but in a relation also to the creator of nature.

What is the Sabbath? *Spirit in the form of time.* With our bodies we belong to space; our spirit, our souls, soar to eternity, aspire to the holy. The Sabbath is an ascent to the summit. It gives us the opportunity to sanctify time, to raise the good to the level of the holy, to behold the holy by abstaining from profanity.

Spirit in the form of time, eternity, is, indeed, an absurdity to all those who think that the spirit is but an idea in the mind of man or that God is a thing among other things. Yet those who realize that God is at least as great as the known universe, that the spirit is an endless process of which we humbly partake, will understand and experience what it means that the spirit is disclosed at certain moments of time. One must be overawed by the marvel of time to be ready to perceive the presence of eternity in a single moment. One must live and act as if the fate of all of time would depend on a single moment.

We usually think that the earth is our mother, that time is money and profit our mate. The seventh day is a reminder that God is our father, that time is life and the spirit our mate.

There is a world of things and a world of spirit. Sabbath is a microcosm of spirit, as if combining in itself all the elements of the macrocosm of spirit.

Just as the physical world does not owe its existence to the power of man—it is simply there—so does the spirit not owe its existence to the mind of man. The Sabbath is not holy by the grace of man. It was God who sanctified the seventh day.

In the language of the Bible the world was brought into being in the six days of creation, yet its survival depends upon the holiness of the seventh day. Great are the laws that govern the processes of nature. Yet without holiness there would be neither greatness nor nature.

IX

Holiness in Time

Holiness in space, in nature, was known in other religions. New in the teaching of Judaism was that the idea of holiness was gradually shifted from space to time, from the realm of nature to the realm of history, from things to events. The physical world became divested of any inherent sanctity.[1] There were no naturally sacred plants or animals any more. To be sacred, a thing had to be consecrated by a conscious act of man. The quality of holiness is not in the grain of matter. It is a preciousness bestowed upon things by an act of consecration and persisting in relation to God.

The emphasis on time is a predominant feature of prophetic thinking. "The day of the Lord" is more important to the prophets than "the house of the Lord."

Mankind is split into nations and divided in states. It is a moment in time—the Messianic end of days—that will give back to man what a thing in space, the Tower of Babel, had taken away. It was the vision of the Messianic day in which the hope of restoring the unity of all men was won.[2]

There is no mention of a sacred place in the Ten Commandments. On the contrary, following the event at Sinai, Moses is told: "In every place where I cause My name to be mentioned I will come unto thee and bless thee" (Exodus 20:24). The awareness that sanctity is not bound to a particular place made possi-

ble the rise of the synagogue. The temple was only in
Jerusalem, while the synagogue was in every village.
There are fixed times, but no fixed place of prayer.

In the Bible, no thing, no place on earth, is holy by
itself. Even the site on which the only sanctuary was to
be built in the Promised Land is never called holy in
the Pentateuch, nor was it determined or specified in
the time of Moses. More than twenty times it is referred to as "the place which the Lord your God *shall
choose.*" [3]

For generations the site remained unknown. But the
king David cherished the aspiration to build a temple
for the Lord. "And it came to pass, when the king
dwelt in his house, and the Lord had given him rest
from all his enemies round about, that the king said
unto Nathan the prophet: 'See now, I dwell in a house
of cedar, but the ark of God dwelleth within cur-
tains.' " [4]

It is of David's eagerness that the Psalmist sings:

Lord, remember unto David
All his affliction;
How he swore unto the Lord
And he vowed unto the Mighty
    One of Jacob:
Surely I will not come into
    the tent of my house,
Nor go up into the bed
    That is spread for me;
I will not give sleep to mine eyes,
Nor slumber to mine eyelids;
Until I find out a place for the Lord,
A dwelling-place for the Mighty One of Jacob . . . [5]

It was in answer to David's prayer that the site for
the temple was made known.

For the Lord hath chosen Zion;
He hath desired it for His habitation:
This is My resting-place for ever.
Here will I dwell; for I have desired it.[6]

The site was chosen not because it was endowed
with any supernatural quality, autochthonous, inherent
in the soil, but because man prayed for it and God desired it.[7]

The temple became a sacred place, yet its sacredness
was not self-begotten. Its sanctity was established, yet
the paradox of a sanctity in space was sensed by the
prophets.

The pious people of Israel would sing:

Let us go into His dwelling-place;
Let us worship at His footstool;[8]

but the prophet proclaimed:

Thus saith the Lord:
The heaven is My throne,
And the earth is My footstool;
Where is the house that ye may build unto Me?
And where is the place that may be My resting-place? [9]

If God is everywhere, He cannot be just somewhere. If
God has made all things, how can man make a thing
for Him? [10] In the Sabbath liturgy, we recite till this
day:

His glory fills the universe.
His angels ask one another:
Where is the place of His glory?

The ancient rabbis discern three aspects of holiness:
the holiness of the Name of God, the holiness of the

Sabbath, and the holiness of Israel.[11] The holiness of the Sabbath preceded the holiness of Israel.[12] The holiness of the Land of Israel is derived from the holiness of the people of Israel.[13] The land was not holy at the time of Terah or even at the time of the Patriarchs. It was sanctified by the people when they entered the land under the leadership of Joshua. The land was sanctified by the people, and the Sabbath was sanctified by God. The sanctity of the Sabbath is not like that of the festivals. The sanctity of the festivals depends upon an act of man. It is man who fixes the calendar and thus determines on which day of the week a festival will come. If the people should fail to establish the beginning of the new month, Passover would not be celebrated. It is different in regard to the Sabbath. Even when men forsake the Sabbath, its holiness remains.[14] And yet all aspects of holiness are mysteriously interrelated.[15]

The sense of holiness in time is expressed in the manner in which the Sabbath is celebrated. No ritual object is required for keeping the seventh day, unlike most festivals on which such objects are essential to their observance, as, for example, unleavened bread, Shofar, Lulab and Etrog or the Tabernacle.[16] On that day the symbol of the Covenant, the phylacteries, displayed on all days of the week, is dispensed with. Symbols are superfluous: the Sabbath is itself the symbol.

"The Sabbath is all holiness." [17] Nothing is essentially required save a soul to receive more soul. For the Sabbath "maintains all souls." [18] It *is* the world of souls: spirit in the form of time. All sages agree, we are told in the Talmud, that the first feast of weeks on which the Torah was given fell on the Sabbath.[19] Indeed, it is the only day on which the word of God could have been given to man.

Every seventh day a miracle comes to pass, the resurrection of the soul, of the soul of man and of the soul of all things. A medieval sage declares: The world which was created in six days was a world without a soul. It was on the seventh day that the world was given a soul. This is why it is said: "and on the seventh day He rested *vayinnafash*" (Exodus 31:17); *nefesh* means a soul.[20]

X

Thou Shalt Covet

The holiness of the chosen day is not something at which to stare and from which we must humbly stay away. It is holy not *away* from us. It is holy *unto* us. *"Ye shall keep the Sabbath therefore, for it is holy unto you"* (Exodus 31:14). "The Sabbath adds holiness to Israel." [1]

What the Sabbath imparts to man is something real, almost open to perception, a light, as it were, that shines from within, that glows out of his face. "God blessed the seventh day" (Genesis 2:3) : "He blessed it with the light of a man's face: The light of a man's face during the week is not the same as it is on the Sabbath." [2] That is an observation made by Rabbi Shimeon ben Yohai.[3]

Something happens to a man on the Sabbath day. On the eve of the Sabbath the Lord gives man *neshamah yeterah,* and at the conclusion of the Sabbath He takes it away from him, says Rabbi Shimeon ben Laqish.[4]

Neshamah yeterah means additional spirit. It is usually translated "additional soul." But what is the strict significance of the term?

Some thinkers took the term *neshamah yeterah* as a figurative expression for increased spirituality or ease and comfort.[5] Others believed that an actual spiritual entity, a second soul, becomes embodied in man on the seventh day. "Man is given on this day an additional, a supernal soul, a soul which is all perfection, according to the pattern of the world to come." [6] It is "the holy spirit that rests upon man and adorns him with a crown like the crown of angels," and is given to every individual according to his attainments.[7]

It is for a spiritual purpose, the Zohar implies, that supernal souls leave their heavenly sphere to enter for a day the lives of mortal men. At every conclusion of the Sabbath day when the supernal souls return to their sphere, they all assemble before the presence of the Holy King. The Holy One, then, asks all the souls: what new insight into the wisdom of the Torah have ye attained while present in the lower world? Happy is the soul that is able to relate in the presence of God an insight attained by man during the seventh day.[8] Indeed, how embarrassed must be the soul which appearing before the presence of God remains mute, having nothing to relate.

According to an ancient legend, the light created at the very beginning of creation was not the same as the light emitted by the sun, the moon, and the stars. The light of the first day was of a sort that would have enabled man to see the world at a glance from one end to the other. Since man was unworthy to enjoy the blessing of such light, God concealed it; but in the world to come it will appear to the pious in all its pristine glory. Something of that light rests upon saints and men of righteous deeds on the seventh day, and that light is called the additional soul.[9]

Legend relates that Rabbi Loew of Prague (died 1609) was called "the Tall Rabbi Loew," because on the Sabbath he looked as if he were a head taller than during the six days of the week.[10] Whoever looked on the Sabbath at Rabbi Hayim of Tshernovitz (died 1813), the story goes, could see a rose on his cheek. The same Rabbi Hayim writes: "We have seen with our own eyes the tremendous change that the holiness of the Sabbath brings about in the life of a saint. The light of holiness blazes in his heart like tongues of fire, and he is overcome with rapture and yearning to serve God . . . all night and all day" . . . As soon as his preparations in honor of the Sabbath are completed "an effulgence of Sabbath-holiness illumines his face. So resplendent is his countenance that one almost hesitates to come close to him." [11]

But the Sabbath as experienced by man cannot survive in exile, a lonely stranger among days of profanity. It needs the companionship of all other days. All days of the week must be spiritually consistent with the Day of Days. All our life should be a pilgrimage to the seventh day; the thought and appreciation of what this day may bring to us should be ever present in our minds. For the Sabbath is the counterpoint of living; the melody sustained throughout all agitations and vicissitudes which menace our conscience; our awareness of God's presence in the world.

What *we are* depends on what *the Sabbath is* to us. The law of the Sabbath day is in the life of the spirit what the law of gravitation is in nature.

Nothing is as hard to suppress as the will to be a slave to one's own pettiness. Gallantly, ceaselessly, quietly, man must fight for inner liberty. Inner liberty depends upon being exempt from domination of things as well as from domination of people. There are many who have acquired a high degree of political and social liberty, but only very few are not enslaved to things. This is our constant problem—how to live with people and remain free, how to live with things and remain independent.

In a moment of eternity, while the taste of redemption was still fresh to the former slaves, the people of

Israel were given the Ten Words, the Ten Commandments. In its beginning and end, the Decalogue deals with the liberty of man. The first Word—*I am the Lord thy God, who brought thee out of the Land of Egypt, out of the house of bondage*—reminds him that his outer liberty was given to him by God, and the tenth Word—*Thou shalt not covet!*—reminds him that he himself must achieve his inner liberty.

When today we wish to bring a word into special prominence we either underline it or print it in italics. In ancient literature, emphasis is expressed through direct repetition (epizeuxis), by repeating a word without any intervening words.[12] The Bible, for example, says: "Justice, Justice shalt thou follow" (Deuteronomy 16:20); "Comfort ye, comfort ye My people" (Isaiah 40:1). Of all the Ten Commandments, only one is proclaimed twice, the last one: "Thou shalt not covet . . . Thou shalt not covet." Clearly it was reiterated in order to stress its extraordinary importance. Man is told not to covet "thy neighbor's house," "thy neighbor's wife, nor his man-servant nor his maid-servant, nor his ox, nor his ass, nor any thing belonging to thy neighbor."

We know that passion cannot be vanquished by decree. The tenth injunction would, therefore, be practically futile, were it not for the "commandment" regarding the Sabbath day to which about a third of the text of the Decalogue is devoted, and which is an epitome of all other commandments. We must seek to find a relation between the two "commandments." Do not covet anything belonging to thy neighbor; I have given thee something that belongs to Me. What is that something? A day.

Judaism tries to foster the vision of life as a pilgrimage to the seventh day; the longing for the Sabbath all days of the week which is a form of longing for the eternal Sabbath all the days of our lives.[13] It seeks to displace the coveting of things in space for *coveting the things in time*, teaching man to covet the seventh day all days of the week. God himself coveted that day, He called it *Hemdat Yamim*, a day to be coveted.[14] It is as if the command: *Do not covet things of space*, were correlated with the unspoken word: *Do covet things of time.*

Epilogue

To Sanctify Time

Pagans project their consciousness of God into a visible image or associate Him with a phenomenon in nature, with a thing of space. In the Ten Commandments, the Creator of the universe identifies Himself by an event in history, by an event in time, the liberation of the people from Egypt, and proclaims: "Thou shalt not make unto thee any graven image or any likeness of any thing that is in heaven above, or that is in the earth, or that is in the water under the earth."

The most precious thing that has ever been on earth were the Two Tablets of stone which Moses received upon Mount Sinai; they were priceless beyond compare. He had gone up into the Mount to receive them; there he abode forty days and forty nights; he did neither eat bread nor drink water. And the Lord delivered unto him the Two Tablets of stone, and on them were written the Ten Commandments, the words which the Lord spoke with the people of Israel in the Mount out of the midst of fire. But when coming down the Mount at the end of forty days and forty nights—the Two Tablets in his hands—Moses saw the people dance around the Golden Calf, he cast the Tablets out of his hands and broke them before their eyes.

"Every important cult-center of Egypt asserted its primacy by the dogma that it was the *site* of creation." [1] In contrast, the book of Genesis speaks of the days rather than of the site of creation.[2] In the myths there is no reference to the time of creation, whereas the Bible speaks of the creation of space in time.

Everyone will admit that the Grand Canyon is more awe-inspiring than a trench. Everyone knows the difference between a worm and an eagle. But how many of us have a similar sense of discretion for the diversity of time? The historian Ranke claimed that every age is equally near to God. Yet Jewish tradition claims that there is a hierarchy of moments within time, that all ages are not alike. Man may pray to God equally at all places, but God does not speak to man equally at all times. At a certain moment, for example, the spirit of prophecy departed from Israel.

Time to us is a measuring device rather than a realm in which we abide. Our consciousness of it comes about when we begin to compare two events and to notice that one event is later than the other; when listening to a tune we realize that one note follows the other. Fundamental to the consciousness of time is the distinction between earlier and later.

But is time only a relation between events in time? Is there no meaning to the present moment, regardless of its relation to the past? Moreover, do we only know what is *in* time, merely events that have an impact on things of space? If nothing happened that is related to the world of space, would there be no time?

A special consciousness is required to recognize the ultimate significance of time. We all live it and are so close to being identical with it that we fail to notice it. The world of space surrounds our existence.[3] It is but a part of living, the rest is time. Things are the shore, the voyage is in time.

Existence is never explicable through itself but only through time. When closing our eyes in moments of intellectual concentration, we are able to have time without space, but we can never have space without time. To the spiritual eye space is frozen time, and all things are petrified events.

There are two points of view from which time can be sensed: from the point of view of space and from the point of view of spirit. Looking out of the window of a swiftly moving railroad car, we have the impression that the landscape is moving while we ourselves are sitting still. Similarly, when gazing at reality while our souls are carried away by spatial things, time appears to be in constant motion. However, when we learn to understand that it is the spatial things that are constantly running out, we realize that time is that which never expires, that it is the world of space which is rolling through the infinite expanse of time. Thus temporality may be defined as the relation of space to time.

The boundless continuous but vacuous entity which realistically is called space is not the ultimate form of reality. Our world is a world of space moving through time—from the Beginning to the End of Days.

To the common mind the essence of time is evanescence, temporality. The truth, however, is that the fact of evanescence flashes upon our minds when poring over things of space. It is the world of space that communicates to us the sense for temporality. Time, that which is beyond and independent of space, is everlasting; it is the world of space which is perishing. Things perish within time; time itself does not change. We should not speak of the flow or passage of time but of the flow or passage of space through time. It is not time that dies; it is the human body which dies in time. Temporality is an attribute of the world of space, of things of space. Time which is beyond space is beyond the division in past, present and future.

Monuments of stone are destined to disappear; days of spirit never pass away. About the arrival of the people at Sinai we read in the Book of Exodus: "In the third month after the children of Israel were gone forth out of the land of Egypt, on *this day* they came into the wilderness of Sinai" (19:1). Here was an expression that puzzled the ancient rabbis: on *this day*? It should have been said: on *that day*. This can only mean that the day of giving the Torah can never become past; that day is this day, every day. The Torah, whenever we study it, must be to us "as if it were given us today." [4] The same applies to the day of the exodus from Egypt: "In every age man must see himself as if he himself went out of Egypt." [5]

The worth of a great day is not measured by the space it occupies in the calendar. Exclaimed Rabbi Akiba: "All of time is not as worthy as the day on which the Song of Songs was given to Israel, for all the songs are holy, but the Song of Songs is the holiest of holies." [6]

In the realm of spirit, there is no difference between a second and a century, between an hour and an age. Rabbi Judah the Patriarch cried: "There are those who gain eternity in a lifetime, others who gain it in one brief hour." [7] One good hour may be worth a lifetime; an instant of returning to God may restore what has been lost in years of escaping from Him. "Better is one hour of repentance and good deeds in this world than the whole life in the world to come." [8]

Technical civilization, we have said, is man's triumph over space. Yet time remains impervious. We can overcome distance but can neither recapture the past nor dig out the future. Man transcends space, and time transcends man.

Time is man's greatest challenge. We all take part in a procession through its realm which never comes to an end but are unable to gain a foothold in it. Its reality is apart and away from us. Space is exposed to our will; we may shape and change the things in space as we please. Time, however, is beyond our reach, beyond our power. It is both near and far, intrinsic to all experience and transcending all experience. It belongs exclusively to God.

Time, then, is *otherness*, a mystery that hovers above all categories. It is as if time and the mind were a world apart. Yet, it is only within time that there is fellowship and *togetherness* of all beings.

Every one of us occupies a portion of space. He takes it up exclusively. The portion of space which my body occupies is taken up by myself in exclusion of anyone else. Yet, no one possesses time. There is no moment which I possess exclusively. This very moment belongs to all living men as it belongs to me. We share time, we own space. Through my ownership of space, I am a rival of all other beings; through my living in time, I am a contemporary of all other beings. We pass through time, we occupy space. We easily succumb to the illusion that the world of space is for our sake, for man's sake. In regard to time, we are immune to such an illusion.

Immense is the distance that lies between God and a thing. For a thing is that which has separate or individual existence as distinct from the totality of beings. To see a thing is to see something which is detached and isolated. A thing is, furthermore, something which is and can become the possession of man. Time does not permit an instant to be in and for itself. Time is either all or nothing. It cannot be divided except in our minds. It remains beyond our grasp. It is almost holy.

It is easy to pass by the great sight of eternal time.

According to the Book of Exodus, Moses beheld his first vision "in a flame of fire, out of the midst of a bush: and he looked, and, behold, the bush burned with fire, and the bush was not consumed" (3:2). Time is like an eternal burning bush. Though each instant must vanish to open the way to the next one, time itself is not consumed.

Time has independent ultimate significance; it is of more majesty and more provocative of awe than even a sky studded with stars. Gliding gently in the most ancient of all splendors, it tells so much more than space can say in its broken language of things, playing symphonies upon the instruments of isolated beings, unlocking the earth and making it happen.

Time is the process of creation, and things of space are results of creation. When looking at space we see the products of creation; when intuiting time we hear the process of creation. Things of space exhibit a deceptive independence. They show off a veneer of limited permanence. Things created conceal the Creator. It is the dimension of time wherein man meets God, wherein man becomes aware that every instant is an act of creation, a Beginning, opening up new roads for ultimate realizations. Time is the presence of God in the world of space, and it is within time that we are able to sense the unity of all beings.

Creation, we are taught, is not an act that happened once upon a time, once and for ever. The act of bringing the world into existence is a continuous process.[9] God called the world into being, and that call goes on. There is this present moment because God is present. Every instant is an act of creation. A moment is not a terminal but a flash, a signal of Beginning. Time is perpetual innovation, a synonym for continuous creation. Time is God's gift to the world of space.

A world without time would be a world without God, a world existing in and by itself, without renewal, without a Creator. A world without time would be a world detached from God, a thing in itself, reality without realization. A world in time is a world going on through God; realization of an infinite design; not a thing in itself but a thing for God.

To witness the perpetual marvel of the world's coming into being is to sense the presence of the Giver in the given, to realize that the source of time is eternity, that the secret of being is the eternal within time.

We cannot solve the problem of time through the conquest of space, through either pyramids or fame. We can only solve the problem of time through sanctification of time. To men alone time is elusive; to men with God time is eternity in disguise.

Creation is the language of God, Time is His song, and things of space the consonants in the song. To sanctify time is to sing the vowels in unison with Him.

This is the task of men: to conquer space and sanctify time.

We must conquer space in order to sanctify time. All week long we are called upon to sanctify life through employing things of space. On the Sabbath it is given us to share in the holiness that is in the heart of time. Even when the soul is seared, even when no prayer can come out of our tightened throats, the clean, silent rest of the Sabbath leads us to a realm of endless peace, or to the beginning of an awareness of what eternity means. There are few ideas in the world of thought which contain so much spiritual power as the idea of the Sabbath. Aeons hence, when of many of our cherished theories only shreds will remain, that cosmic tapestry will continue to shine.

Eternity utters a day.

Notes

Prologue

[1] See A. J. Heschel, *Man Is Not Alone.* A Philosophy of Religion, New York 1951, p. 200.

[2] According to Bertrand Russell, time is "an unimportant and superficial characteristic of reality . . . A certain emancipation from slavery to time is essential to philosophic thought . . . To realize the unimportance of time is the gate of wisdom." *Our Knowledge of the External World, pp.* 166-67.

[3] "Time is an evil, a mortal disease, exuding a fatal nostalgia. The passage of time strikes a man's heart with despair, and fills his gaze with sadness." N. Berdyaev, *Solitude and Society,* p. 134.

[4] See also A. J. Heschel, *The Earth Is the Lord's,* p. 13f.

[5] This is one of the aspects which distinguishes the religious from the esthetic experience.

[6] Maimonides, *Mishneh Torah, Teshubah* 1,3, on the basis of *Mishnah Yoma,* 8,8. A more radical view is found in *Sifra* to 23:27, and *Shebuot* 13a (the Soncino translation) : "I might think that the Day of Atonement should not atone unless he fasted on it, and called it a holy convocation (by including in the prayers of that day: Blessed art thou, O Lord . . . who sanctifiest Israel and the Day of Atonement; and by wearing holiday garments to signify his acceptance of the Day as holy; see *Tosafot Keritot* 7a), and did no work on it. But if he did not fast on it, and did not call it a holy convocation, and worked on it —whence do we deduce (that the Day atones for him)? Scripture says, It is a Day of Atonement—in all cases it atones." However, the view that the Day atones even for those who do not repent but actually sin on the very Day is not shared by most authorities. Compare also the opinion of Rabbi, *Yoma* 85b.—Significant is Rabbi Yose's con-

ception of special times, *Sanhedrin* 102a. See also *Tanhuma* to Genesis 49:28.

See also the views expressed by Rabbi Yohanan in *Ta'anit* 29a and by Rabbi Yose in *Erachin* 11b. Also Pedersen, *Israel I-II*, p. 488 and p. 512; E. Panofsky, *Studies in Iconology*, pp. 69-93.

[7] Genesis 2:3. "Remember the Sabbath *day*, to keep it *holy*. . . . for in six days the Lord made heaven and earth . . . wherefore the Lord blessed the Sabbath *day* and made it *holy*" (Exodus 20:8.11). In the Ten Commandments, the term *holy* is applied to one word only, the Sabbath.

[8] See *Tanhuma*, Exodus 34:1 (31); *Seder 'Olam rabba*, ch. 6. Rashi to Exodus 31:18. See, however, Nahmanides to Leviticus 8:2.

Holiness of time would have been sufficient to the world. Holiness of space was a necessary comprise with the nature of man. The erection of a tabernacle was not commanded in the Decalogue. It was begun in answer to a direct appeal from the people who pleaded with God: "O Lord of the world! The kings of the nations have palaces in which are set a table, candlesticks and other royal insignia that their king may be recognized as such. Shall not Thou, too, our King, Redeemer and Helper, employ royal insignia, that all the dwellers of the earth may recognize that Thou art their King?" *Midrash Aggada* 27:1; Louis Ginzberg, *The Legends of the Jews*, III, 148f.

[9] Numbers 7:1.

[10] Each revolution from one new moon to the next constitutes a lunar month and measures about 29 days and 12 hours.

[11] The Babylonian seventh day was observed on every seventh day of the lunar month; see J. Barth, *The Jewish Sabbath and the Babylonians*, *The American Israelite*, Nov. 20, 1902; also H. Webster, *Rest Days*, New York, 1916, p. 253f.

Chapter I

[1] Philo, *De Specialibus Legibus*, II,60 (Loeb Classics, Philo, VII).

[2] *Ethica Nicomachea* X,6.

[3] Rabbi Solomo Alkabez, *Lechah Dodi*.

[4] The Evening Service for the Sabbath.

[5] *Zohar*, I, 75.

[6] H. O. Taylor, *The Medieval Mind*, I, p. 588 ff.

[7] *Mekilta* to 31:13.

[8] *Genesis rabba* 19,3.

[9] Except the prohibition of idolatry, adultery and murder.

[10] *Otzar ha-Geonim, Yoma,* p. 30,32.

[11] *Duas tantum res anxius optat, panem et circenses,* Juvenal, *Satires* X.80.

[12] The Afternoon Prayer for the Sabbath.

[13] Isaiah 58:13. "He who diminishes the delight of the Sabbath, it is as if he robbed the Shechniah, for the Sabbath is (God's) only daughter," *Tikkune Zohar* 21, ed. Mantua 1558, 59b.

[14] *Deuteronomy rabba* 3,1; see *Midrash Tehillim,* chap. 90.

[15] See *Toledot Ya'akob Yosef,* Koretz, 1760, p. 203c.

[16] Therefore we say on the Sabbath . . . "Rejoice O heavens, be glad O earth" (Psalms 96:11). "Heavens symbolizes the world to come, the world of souls, while earth symbolizes this world which is earthly and mortal." Al Nakawa, *Menorat ha-Maor,* ed. Enelow, II, 182.

[17] *Shibbole ha-Leqet,* chap. 126.

[18] The Afternoon Prayer for the Sabbath.

[19] Jer. *Demai* II, 23d.

[20] *Zohar,* 88b. cf. 128a.

[21] Rabbi Zvi Elimelech of Dynow, *Bne Issachar,* Shabbat, 1.

[22] B. Auerbach, *Poet and Merchant,* New York, 1877, p. 27.

[23] Quoted as a Midrash by Rashi on *Megillah* 9a; on Genesis 2:2; *Tosafot Sanhedrin* 38a.

According to the hellenistic Jewish philosopher, Aristobulus, on the seventh day was created the light in which all things can be seen, namely the light of wisdom. See Eusebius, *Praeparatio Evangelica,* ed. Gifford, Book XIII, chap. 12, 667a.

[24] *Genesis rabba* 10,9.

[25] Deuteronomy 12:9; cf. Kings 8:56; Psalms 95:11; Ruth 1:19.

[26] Job 3:13.17; cf. 14:13 ff.

[27] Psalms 23:1-2.

[28] *Shabbat* 152b; see also *Kuzari* V,10; *Yalkut Reubeni,* Amsterdam, 1700, 174a, and the prayer *El male rahamim.*

[29] See *Shabbat* 119b.

[30] Wertheimer, *Batei Midrashot,* Jerusalem, 1950, p. 27; see L. Ginzberg, *Legends of the Jews,* I, 85; V, 110.

[31] *Or Zarua,* II, 18c. See the emendation suggested by L. Ginzberg, *The Legends of the Jews,* V, 101; *Geonica* II, 48. Compare, however, the beautiful legend in *Yalkut Shimoni,* Tehillim, 843.

Chapter II

[1] Exodus 20:9; 23:12; 31:15; 34:21; Leviticus 23:3; Deuteronomy 5:13.
[2] *Mekilta de-Rabbi Shimeon ben Yohai,* ed. Hoffmann, Frankfurt a.M. 1905, p. 107.
[3] *Pirke Abot* 1,10.
[4] *Abot de-Rabbi Natan,* ed. Schechter, chap. 11.
[5] See *Shabbat* 49b.
[6] Rabbi Isaiah Horowitz, *Shne Luhot ha-Berit,* Frankfurt a.d. Oder, 1717, p. 131a.
[7] *Shabbat* 12a.
[8] "Rabbi Sheshet used to place his scholars in a place exposed to the sun in summer, and in a shady place in winter, so that they should arise quickly (when he lectured to them on the Sabbath). Rabbi Zera used to seek out pairs of scholars (engaged in learned discussion) and say to them, 'I beg of you do not profane it' (the Sabbath, by neglecting its delights and good cheer)." *Shabbat* 119a-b.
[9] Al Nakawa, *Menorat ha-Maor,* II, 191.
[10] *Sefer Hasidim,* ed. Wistinetzki, Berlin, 1924, p. 426; see Jer. *Berachot* 5b.
[11] Deuteronomy 5:15.
[12] K. Kamelhar, *Dor De'ah,* Bilgoraj, 1933, p. 127.
[13] Mekilta to 20:9.
According to Edward Mahler, the verb "shabbat" does not mean "to rest" but "to be complete." *Shabbatu,* the noun, means in Babylonian a cycle in a chronological sense, the day on which the moon completes its cycle, the day of the full moon. *Der Schabbat,* ZDMG, LXII, 33-79.
[14] Jer. *Shabbat* 15a.

Chapter III

[1] *Shabbat* 33b and the version and English translation in *Maaseh Book,* translated by Moses Gaster, Jewish Publication Society, Philadelphia, 1934, p. 25 ff.
[2] Cf. e.g., J. H. Weiss, *"Zur Geschichte der Jüdischen Tradition"* (Hebrew), II, 143.
[3] Friedlaender, *Roman Life and Manners,* London, 1908, I, 6.
[4] See, for example, the inscription on the tomb of Midas, Di-

ogenes Laertius, *Lives of Eminent Philosophers*, ed. Loeb,
I. 99 f: "I am a maiden of bronze and I rest upon Midas's
tomb. So long as water shall flow and tall trees grow, and
the sun shall rise and shine, and the bright moon, and
rivers shall run and the sea wash the shore, here abiding
on his tear-sprinkled tomb I shall tell the passers-by—
Midas is buried here." A similar view is implied in Joshua
4:7.

[5] The designation *urbs aeterna* occurs already in Tibullus,
and in the *Fasti of Ovid* (3, 78) and frequently in the official documents of the Empire, see *Thesaurus Linguae
Latinae*, I, 1141. Jerusalem is never called *'ir 'olam*. In the
Hellenistic period the epithet eternal is emphatically applied to God, *ribbon ha-'olamin*, θεός (κύριος, βασιλεὺς)
αἰώνιος. See W. Bousset, *Die Religion des Judentums*, 3 ed.,
Tübingen 1936, p. 311, n. 5. We find, however, the expression *'am 'olam*, Isaiah 44:7; Ezechiel 36:20, and the blessing in Jeremiah 17:25. The expression for cemetery, *bet
'olam*, Ecclesiastes 12:5, is an ancient Oriental phrase.

[6] Similar criticism of the Roman government was expressed
in the circle of Rabbi Yohanan ben Zakkai, *Baba Batra*
10b; see also *Pesikta de-Rav Kahana* 95b. Praise of the
Roman Empire is expressed by Rabbi Shimeon ben Laqish,
Genesis Rabba 9,13.

[7] W. W. Fowler, *The Religious Experience of the Roman
People*, p. 387; G. F. Moore, *History of Religions*, I, 551.
See especially Erwin Rohde, *Psyche*, Tübingen 1925, II, p.
336 ff.

[8] Rohde, *Psyche*, II, p. 395.

[9] *Philippics*, XIV, 12. According to an old maxim,
"pleasures are transient, honors are immortal," Diogenes
Laertius, 1.97.

[10] *Mihi populus Romanus aeternitatem immortalitatemquem
donavit, Oratio in Pisonem*, 7. About Cicero's true attitude
toward the problem of immortality, see Rohde, l.c., p.
326, 1.

[10a] *Epistolae Morales* (Loeb Classics) C11, 29. See A. Kamin-
ka, in *Sefer Klausner*, Tel Aviv, 1937, p. 172.

[11] Isaiah 40:6.8.

[12] See the statement by Rabbi Akiba who was Rabbi
Shimeon's teacher in *Abot* 3, 14.

[13] The blessing recited after reading the Torah.

[14] *Pesikta*, ed. Buber, p. 39 b.

Chapter IV

[1] Jer. *Hagigah* 77b.

[2] Jer. *Hagigah* 77b.

[3] *Abot de-Rabbi Natan*, chap. 28.

[4] *Berachot* 35b.

[5] See J. G. Frazer, *The Myths of the Origin of Fire*, London, 1930, p. 193 f.

[6] *Bet Midrash*, V, 153.

[7] *Mishneh Torah, Ishut* 10,4.

[8] Rashi, *Shabbat* 150b.

[9] *Mishnah Sotah* 9,14; *Tosefta* 15,8; *Talmud* 49b.
The Hebrew word for myrtle *hadassah* was the original name for beautiful Esther (Esther 2:7). In Halevi's poetry, the bride is described as "a flowing myrtle tree among the trees of Eden." See I. Löw, *Die Flora der Juden*, II, 273. In Greek mythology, the myrtle is Aphrodite's special plant and a symbol of love. Pauly Wissowa, s.v. Aphrodite, p. 2767; s.v. Myrtle, p. 1179.

[10] *Ketubot* 17a. Rabbi Samuel the son of Rabbi Isaac danced with three twigs. Said Rabbi Zera: The old man is putting us to shame. When Rabbi Samuel died, a pillar of fire appeared, separating him from the rest of the world. And there is a tradition that a pillar of fire establishes such a separation only for one or two men in a generation. See also Jer. *Peah* 15d; Jer. *Abodah Zara* 42c.

[11] The myrtle came to be considered as the plant of the Sabbath ("The Sabbath needs the myrtle," *Sefer Hasidim*, ed. Wistinetzki, Frankfurt a.M., 1924, 553, p. 145). Following Rabbi Isaac Luria, many people would take on Friday evening two bunches of myrtle, recite the benediction over them and smell their fragrance. See *Shulhan Aruch* of Rabbi Isaac Luria, Wilno, 1880, p. 29a; see also Rabbi Isaiah Horowitz, *Shne Luhot ha-Berit*, Frankfurt a.d. Oder, 1717, p. 133b. Lauterbach's explanation of the use of the myrtle on the Sabbath, *Hebrew Union College Annual*, XV, 393f, is incongruous with its role in the story of Rabbi Shimeon ben Yohai.

At the conclusion of the Sabbath, when the additional soul departs, one must be refreshed by smelling aromatic herbs, for at that moment "the soul and the spirit are separated and sad until the smell comes and unites them and makes them glad." *Zohar* III, p. 35 b. According to

Ibn Gabbai, *Tola'at Jacob*, p. 30a, the myrtle is preferable for that purpose. Compare the other sources cited by Lauterbach, *Hebrew Union College Annual*, XV, 382f. The Talmud speaks always of the use of aromatic herbs for the *habdalah* ceremony and never refers specifically to the myrtle. To this day, the custom of reciting the blessing over aromatic herbs contained in a spice box during the *habdalah* is common.

12 Following the statement of "the old man" that he was holding two bundles of myrtle in honor of the Sabbath (see above, p. 37), Rabbi Shimeon asked him: "But one should suffice you?" The old man replied: "One is for 'Remember' and one for 'Keep.'" This was an allusion to the two different words with which the commandment of the Sabbath begins in the two versions of the Ten Commandments (Exodus 20:8 and Deuteronomy 5:12). According to an old mystic text, "Remember" is a reference to the male principle, "Keep" to the female principle, *Bahir*, Wilna, 1913, p. 17d. This we may assume suggested to Rabbi Shimeon the idea that the Sabbath was the bride and Israel the bridegroom.

Chapter V

1 *Genesis rabba* 11,8. The interpretation offered here is allegorical; compare *Beure Hagra*, Gaon of Wilna, Warsaw, 1886, p. 98. Israel's relationship to God is partly an open fact of history and partly a mystery, an intimate act. To Rabbi Shimeon ben Yohai, the Sabbath is the sign of the mystery in that relationship. Says he: All mitzvot, all commandments, the Holy One gave to Israel in public, except the Sabbath which was given in privacy, as it is written *between Me and Israel it is a sign for Israel le-'olam,* (Exodus 31:17). *Between . . . and* is a Hebrew expression for intimacy of husband and wife (cf. *Nedarim* 79b). The word *le-'olam* (for ever) is written in such a way that it may be read as if it were vocalized *le-'alem:* to be kept as a secret (*Bezah* 16a).

2 *Shabbat* 119a. Rabbi Yannai's first residence was in Sephoris. Later rabbis found an allusion to the idea of the Sabbath as a bride in the world *vaykullu* (Genesis 2:1). *Lekah Tob*, ed. Buber, Wilna, 1884, p. 9a. Cf. the quotation from *Midrash Hashkem* in Al Nakawa, II, 191.

³ Rabbenu Hananel, *Baba Kama* 32a. Cf. R. Rabinowicz, *Variae lectiones, ad locum.*

⁴ *Shabbat* 119a. Rabbi Hanina ben Hama of Sephoris died about the year 250. There is, or course, no inconsistency in calling the Sabbath both "bride" and "queen." An old Hebrew proverb states "the groom is like a king." *Pirke de Rabbi Eliezer,* chap. 16, end. Specifically it is said in *Zohar, Raya Mehemna,* III, 272b: "The Sabbath is both queen and bride."—If the day is a bride, who is the king? In the utterances of the scholars just quoted, it is left unsaid. To Rabbi Shimeon ben Yohai, however, the Sabbath is the mate of Israel. Yet, in the course of time, the idea assumed a new connotation. Indeed, Rabbi Yohanan, a scholar of the third century, speaks of the Sabbath as being the queen of God. See *Deuteronomy rabba* 1,18; *Exodus rabba* 25,11. Rabbi Yohanan, the famous head of the Academy in Tiberias, who died about the year 279, was a disciple of Rabbi Hanina the Great (see Jer. *Baba Metzia,* chap. 2, end; Bab. *Niddah* 20b) and of Rabbi Yannai (*Baba Batra* 154b; *Yebamot* 92b).

The famous Palestinian homilitician of the third century, Rabbi Levi, a pupil or a contemporary of Rabbi Yohanan, adopted the same metaphor. He explained why a boy is not circumcised until the eighth day: it is like a king who entered a province and issued a decree, saying: "Let no visitors that are here see my face until they have first seen the face of my lady." The lady is the Sabbath. Since there can be no seven continuous days without a Sabbath, the child is exposed to the covenant of the Sabbath before it is entered into the covenant of circumcision. *Leviticus rabba* 27,10. In subsequent ages the second conception prevailed: the Sabbath is the bride, and God is like the groom. The Sabbath is the union of the bride with her heavenly spouse. Rabbi David Abudraham who lived at Seville, Spain, about 1340, says: Because the Sabbath and the Community of Israel are the Bride and God is the Groom, we pray: Grant us that we may be like Thy bride, and that Thy bride may find tranquility in Thee, as it is said in *Ruth rabba:* a woman finds nowhere tranquility except in her husband. Abudraham, Prague, 1784, 44c; see also 45a. The Midrash referred to is probably *Ruth rabba,* 1,15 to 3,1. See Rabbi Moses ben Abraham Katz, *Matteh Mosheh,* chap. 450. This is also the way in which the term "bride" in *Lechah Dodi* is usually understood, see the quotation in *Yessod ve-Shoresh ha-Abodah,* Jerusalem, 1940, *p.* 164. See also *Tikkune Shabbat,* Dyhernfurth, 1692, f. 28. The Sabbath is a synonym for the Shechinah, for the presence of God in the world, *Zohar,* III, 257a. See *Bahir,* Wilna, 1912, p. 17c. Rashi, the classical commentator, afraid lest the feminine metaphor led to misunderstandings, tried to rob it of any literal meaning by changing either the gender or the object of the metaphor. Rabbi Hanina, he said, behaved "like one who goes out to meet a *King*" (*Baba Kama* 32a). Or: "Out of affection he calls the *celebration* of the Sabbath 'queen' " (*Shabbat* 119a)! Similarly, Rashi states that Rab Nahman bar Isaac welcomed the Sabbath "like one who welcomes his teacher" (*Shabbat* 119a). See also Al Nakawa, *Menorat ha-Maor,* III, 586. Maimonides, *Mishneh Torah, Shabbat* 30,2, employs likewise the term "king."

It was the prophet Hosea who was the first to use the idea of romantic love and marriage in describing God's relationship to Israel. God, according to him, is wedded to His people, loving it as a husband loves his wife (3:1). Yet it was another prophet who was the first to compare that relationship with the love of a groom for his bride: "As the bridegroom rejoiceth over the bride, so shall thy God rejoice over thee" (Isaiah 62:5). Rabbi Berachiah enumerates ten places in Scripture in which God refers to Israel as a bride, *Deuteronomy rabba* 2,26; *Canticles rabba,* 4:21; see *Pesikta de- Rab Kahana,* ed. Buber, p. 147b.

That idea became a power in the history of the Jewish soul. It endowed the life of piety with superhuman poetry. It found its culmination in the interpretation of the greatest love song man has ever known: *the Song of Songs.* The Song of Songs assumed only one meaning: that of a dialogue between Israel, the bride of God, and her Beloved; an allegory of the history of Israel from the exodus from Egypt to the time when Messiah will come. On that subject see Salfeld, *Das Hohelied Salomo's bei den jüdischen Erklärern des Mittelalters,* Berlin, 1879; S. Lieberman, *Yemenite Midrashim* (Hebrew), Jerusalem, 1940, p. 12.

The event at Sinai is described as an act of God's betrothal to Israel, *Deuteronomy rabba* 3, 12. *And Moses brought forth the people out of the camp to meet God.* (Exodus 19:17). Said Rabbi Yose: *The Lord came from Sinai* (Deuteronomy 33:2) "to receive Israel as a bridegroom comes forth to meet the bride" (*Mekilta* to 19:17).

Compare Ziegler, *Die Königsgleichnisse des Midrasch,* Breslau, 1903, chap. 10.

There is, however, an essential difference in the way the metaphor of the bride is used by the rabbis from the way it was used by the prophet. In the declaration of the prophet, Israel is called the bride, and the initiative, the attention, is on the part of God. In the words of the rabbis, not Israel but the Sabbath is the bride, and the initiative, the attention, must come from man.

[5] See above, p. 22.

[6] Geniba was a contemporary of Abba Arika who died in the year 247, see Jer. *Abodah Zarah* II, 42a.

[7] *Genesis rabba* 10,9.

[8] See *Exodus rabba* 41,6.

[9] Al Nakawa, *Menorat ha-Maor,* 2, p. 191. "The Sabbath is actually wedded to Israel and the ceremony of the Sabbath eve is like the wedding-ceremony, namely the leading of the bride into the chamber. The Sabbath is also called Queen because of her being a royal bride: all Israelites are princes. This is why at sunset of the Sabbath Rabbi Hanina would exclaim: Come, let us go out to welcome the queen Sabbath, because it is the manner of the groom to go forth to welcome the bride. While the manner of Rabbi Yannai was different, he would not say let us go forth to welcome the bride, but, on the contrary, he would remain on his place and when she arrived he would say: Come in, bride; Come in, bride. Just as the bride arrives after the ceremony from the house of her father at the house of her husband." Rabbi Samuel Edels (1555-1631), Baba Kama 32b.

Chapter VI

[1] The Falashas did personify the Sabbath. To them the Sabbath is God's favorite angel whom all the other angels adore and to whom they chant a song; see Louis Ginzberg, *The Legends of the Jews,* V, 110. On the general problem of hypostatization in Judaism see Paul Heinisch, *Personifikationen und Hypostasen im Alten Testament und im Alten Orient,* Münster, 1921; and W. Bousset, *Die Religion des Judentums im Späthellenistischen* Zeitalter, 3. ed., pp. 342-357.

[2] Rabbi Joshua ben Hanania said: When a festival falls after the Sabbath (beginning Saturday evening) two blessings

must be said, one with which we bid farewell to the Sabbath (*habdalah*) and one with which we welcome the festival (*kiddush*); first we must recite the habdalah and then the kiddush. Explained Rabbi Hanina the reason for this order: The hour on which the Sabbath ends and the festival begins is to be compared to a king who departs from a city and to a governor who then enters it; first you escort the king, and then you go forth to greet the governor. *Pesahim* 103a.

3 R. Meir Ibn Gabbai, *Tola'at Jacob*, Warsaw, 1876, pp. 49, 38. Cf. the same reference in *ha-Manhig*, 70; *Machsor Vitri*, p. 116; *Or Zarua*, Zitomir, 1862, II, 49b. The custom is perhaps indicated in the passage, quoted in fn.2 of this chapter.

4 *Abot* 1, 15; 3,12.

5 *Halakot Gedolot*, p. 206, see I. Mahrschen, *Jeschurun*, Berlin, 1922, IX, 46. Cf. also *Or Zarua*, II, 9b.

6 "When the Sabbath arrives, we receive him with song and melody." *Midrash Tehillim*, ed. Buber, chap. 92, p. 403. The generally accepted view that the service of welcoming the Sabbath, including the reading of Psalms 95, 96, 97, 98, 99 and 29, was first instituted toward the end of the sixteenth century by the Kabbalists of Safed (I. Elbogen, *Der Jüdische Gottesdienst*, p. 108) is open to question. Already Al Nakawa, who lived in Spain and who was killed in the year 1391, mentions the custom of reciting Psalm 96 at the arrival of the Sabbath, which he calls *movaeh Shabbat*, (a term unknown to me from any other source; it apparently corresponds to *motzaeh Shabbat*), see *Menorat ha-Maor*, II, 182. The choice of the particular Psalms may be explained with the reference to the kingship of God found in all these Psalms. The idea of the Sabbath as a queen is an allusion to the kingship of God. The song in the Musaf service: "They that keep the Sabbath, they that call it a delight shall rejoice in Thy kingdom" (*Siddur Saadia*, p. 112), may also be an allusion to the same idea.

Chapter VII

1 *Sefer Hasidim*, vulgata, § 54.

2 *Shabbat* 25b. According to some Kabbalists, the reason for the washing of hands and feet on the eve of the Sabbath is that we are like the priests at the temple in Jerusalem who

were required to perform such ceremonial washing of their hands and feet before they began the sacred service.

3 *Zohar*, III, 136b. Quotations in this chapter are from the Friday Evening Service, except the one from the Song of Songs, 8:6.7.

Chapter VIII

1 "The Seventh day is the sign of the resurrection and the world to come," and there shall therefore be no mourning on that day. *Vita Adae et Evae*, 41.1, *The Apocrypha and Pseudopigrapha*, ed. Charles, II, 151. According to Louis Ginzberg, *The Book of Adam, Jewish Encyclopedia*, the book is of purely Jewish origin.

2 Alphabet of R. Akiba, *Otzar Midrashim*, p. 407; see also p. 430. Cf. also the Midrash quoted in *Kad ha-Qemah, Shabbat, end.*

3 *Mekilta to Exodus* 31:17.

4 *Mishnah Tamid*, end. Cf. *Rosh Hashanah* 31a, where this Mishnah is ascribed to Rabbi Akiba.

5 *Abot de-Rabbi Natan*, chap. 1, where the final passage is found. The description of the world to come is also transmitted in the name of Rab. *Berachot* 17a. See also *Midrash Tehillim*, chap. 92, ed. Buber, p. 201a.

6 Rabbi Solomon of Karlin.

7 See above p. 41.

8 On the Sabbath a prayer is said at the end of grace: "May the All-merciful *let us inherit* the day which will be all Sabbath and rest in the life eternal." Solicitude for eternal life is not brought to expression in the daily liturgy (see *Kuzari* III, 20). Yet in the central prayer for the Sabbath (*the Amidah*), which is read four times, we read the phrase: "Lord, our God, let us inherit Thy holy Sabbath," This is perhaps a reference to the Sabbath as a synonym for the life to come, since the earthly Sabbath is, of course, already in the possession of man.

9 Rabbi Elijah De Vidas, *Reshit Hokmah, Sha'ar ha-qedushah*, ch. 2.

Chapter IX

1 The phrase *Holy Spring* (*he-Aviv ha Qadosh*), used as a title of a book published in 1947 in *Tel Aviv* is a gross spiritual anachronism.

[2] Hermann Cohen, *Jüdische Schriften*, Berlin, 1924, I, 325.

[3] Deuteronomy 12:5. 11.14.18.21.26; 14:23. 24. 25; 15:20; 16:2.6.7.11.15.16; 17:8.10; 23:17; 31:11.

[4] II Samuel 7: 1-2.

[5] Psalms 132: 1-5.

[6] Psalms 132: 13.14.

[7] Later rabbinic tradition claimed that on the spot where the temple was erected several important events took place (see Maimonides, *Mishne Torah, Bet ha-Behirah* II,2). Yet there is no reference to these events in the biblical account. See M. Buber, *Ben Am le-Artzo* (Hebrew), Jerusalem, 1945, p.2.

[8] Psalms 132:7.

[9] Isaiah 66:1.

[10] Cf. Isaiah 66:2.

[11] *Yalkut Shimoni* I, 830. See the Midrash quoted in *Tosafot Hagigah* 3b.

[12] This is why on the festivals we conclude the Haftora benediction: "Who sanctified Israel and the times," while on the Sabbath we conclude: "Who sanctified the Sabbath," —"because the Sabbath preceded Israel"; it came with the creation of the world, *Soferim* 13,14.

[13] See *Mekilta* to 12:1; *Eduyot* 8,6; *Mishneh Torah, Terumot* 1,5; *Tosafot Zebahim* 62a.

[14] "And Moses declared unto the children of Israel the set feasts of the Lord" (Leviticus 23:44). "Only the festivals need sanctification by the Bet Din (the rabbinic courts which must declare which day is a new moon, when the new month begins and thus fix the day upon which the festival will occur), not the Sabbath" (*Nedarim* 78b). See *Mekilta* to 31:15.

[15] Boldly a Midrash declares: "The holiness of God, the holiness of the Sabbath, the holiness of Israel, all these are like one." *Seder Eliyahu Rabba*, ed. M. Friedman, Wien, 1902, p. 133. *Yalkut Shimoni*, I, 833, reads: "The name of God." It is perhaps an allusion to Isaiah 6:3—The sanctity of the Sabbath day was so keenly felt that for the nonobservance of its laws, the Bible had only one name: *hilel*. *Hilel* means to pollute, to defile, to profane the holy. It is a term for desecration; cf. Exodus 31:14; Isaiah 56; 2.6; Ezekiel 20:13.16.21.24; 22:8; 23:38; Nehemiah 13:17.18.

[16] A ritual object is one which serves no other function than that of ritual. The wine and the bread over which the sanctification of the day is recited are neither sacramental nor ritual objects.

[17] *Numbers rabba* 14,5.
[18] *Bahir*, ed. Wilna, 1913, p. 7a.
[19] See *Shabbat* 86b.
[20] Rabbi Solomon ben Abraham Adret of Barcelona (1235-1310) in *En Ya'akob, Taanit* 27b. The idea is implied in *Bahir*, ed. Wilna, 1913, p. 7a and 15b. Cf. the commentary by Rabbi Moshe Alsheikh to Genesis 2:7.

Chapter X

[1] *Mekilta* to 31:14.
[2] *Genesis rabba* 11,2.
[3] See *Mekilta* to 20:11.
[4] *Bezah* 16a; *Ta'anit* 27b. The author of that saying is Rabbi Shimeon ben Laqish, who lived in the third century. See above, chap. 5, n. 11.
[5] Rashi, the classical commentator of the eleventh century, gives it a psychological interpretation. To him, it is "the enhanced receptivity of the soul for quietness, joy and the partaking of food as well as the absence of any feeling of disgust. *Bezah* 16a; see his remark to *Taanit* 27b. The text of Rabbenu Hananel in *Bezah* 16a is apparently corrupt. A more metaphysical conception is given by Ibn Ezra, the rationalist contemporary of Rashi, who claims that on the seventh day there is an actual increase in the intellectual power of the soul. See his commentary to Genesis 2:3. A somewhat similar view is found in Rabbi Menahem Meiri, *Book of Repentance* (Hebrew), ed. A. Schreiber, New York, 1950, p. 531. Even the great mystic Nahmanides is opposed to taking literally the concept of the additional soul; see his *Commentary* to Genesis 2:2; Similarly Rabbi Menashe ben Israel, *Nishmat Hayim*, Amsterdam, 1652, p. 53b. The Italian exegete, physician and philosophical author, Rabbi Obadiah Sforno (1475-1550) characterizes the additional soul as the enhanced capacity of man to attain that which God had willed that he attain when He said "Let us make man in our image, after our likeness", *Commentary* to Exodus 31:17. See also Meyer Waxman in *Sefer Hashanah*, vol. VIII-IX, p. 210f, New York 1947.
[6] *Zohar* II, p. 88b.
[7] *Zohar Hadash*, Genesis, 17b; *Zohar* III, p. 242b. A scholar of the thirteenth century, Rabbi Zedakiah ben Abraham Anan of Rome, says specifically: "On the Sabbath there are two souls in a man." *Shibbole ha-Leqet*, 130. According

to the *Maaseh Book* translated by M. Gaster, p. 305, "Man has one more soul on the Sabbath day than on a week day, and this can be easily observed in the fact that one is more carefree on the Sabbath than on any day of the week".

8 *Zohar III*, p. 173a.

9 Rabbi Aaron Samuel ben Moses Shalom of Kremnitz (died 1616), *Nishmat Adam*, Pietrkow, 1911, p. 24.

10 A similar legend is told about Rabbi Joshua Horowitz, see *Nezir ha-Shem*, Lemberg, 1869, in the preface.

11 *Sidduro shel Shabbat*, Warsaw 1872, p. 8c.

12 Direct repetition is used today in rhetoric: He expressed a new idea—an idea of great significance.

13 The awareness of the spirit of the Sabbath is not restricted to one seventh of the week. The Ten Commandments are found in two versions: in the Book of Exodus and in the Book of Deuteronomy. In the first version the commandment of the Sabbath begins with the words: *Remember* (*zahor*) the seventh day, and in the second: *Keep* (*shamor*) the seventh day. Said a medieval sage: "*Remember* it always, wait for its arrival (*shemor* means also to wait eagerly) . . . Wait, look forward to it like one who looks forward to meeting a person he loves." (Al Nakawa, *Menorat ha-Maor*, III, 575).

14 In the Sabbath liturgy we say: "Thou wast pleased with the seventh day and dist sanctify it, the most coveted of days didst Thou call it." Where in the Bible is the Sabbath called "the most coveted of days"? The verse in Genesis 2:2, which we usually translate: "and God completed on the seventh day," reads in an ancient Aramaic version: "and God coveted the seventh day." See M. Ginsburger, *Das Fragmententhargum* (Targum Jeruschalmi zum Pentateuch), Berlin, 1899.

Epilogue

1 J. A. Wilson, "Egyptian Myths, Tales and Mortuary Texts," in *Ancient Near Eastern Texts*, p. 8.

2 The Legend of the *eben shetiyah* is of post-Biblical origin, cf. Louis Ginzberg, *The Legends of the Jews*, V, 14-16. *Maqom* as an appellation for God in rabbinic literature does not imply the deification of space but, on the contrary, the subordination of space to the divine. Space is not the ultimate; it is transcended by God.

[3] See A. J. Heschel, *Man Is Not Alone, A Philosophy of Religion,* p. 200.

[4] *Tanhuma,* ed. Buber, II, 76; see Rashi to Exodus 19:1; Deuteronomy 26:16.

[5] *Mishnah Pessahim* 10,5.

[6] *Yadayim* 3,5.

[7] *Abodah Zarah* 10b, 17a, 18a.

[8] *Abot* 4,22.

[9] In the daily morning service we read: "The Lord of marvels, in His goodness He renews the wonders of creation every day, constantly." The preservation of the world or the laws that account for the preservation of the world are due to an act of God. "Thou art the Lord, even Thou alone; Thou hast made heaven, the heaven of heavens with all their hosts, the earth and all things that are thereon, the seas and all that is in them, and *Thou preservest them all*" (Nehemiah 9:6). "How manifold are Thy works, O Lord . . . All of them wait for Thee, that Thou mayest give them their food in due season . . . Thou hidest Thy face, they vanish . . . Thou sendest forth Thy spirit, they are created" (Psalms 104:24.27.29.30). Note the present tense in Isaiah 48:13; 42:5; see also, 48:7. Job 34: 14-16; *Kuzari* 3, 11. On seeing the wonders of nature we pray: "Blessed art Thou . . . who performs the wonders of creation" (*Mishnah Berachot* 9,2; see the opinion of Resh Laqish, *Hagigah* 12b and Rashi ad locum). The idea of continuous creation seems to have been the theme of an ancient controversy. According to the School of Shammai, the benediction over the lights which is said at the outgoing of the Sabbath, is: "Blessed art Thou who *created* the lights of fire"; whereas, according to the school of Hillel, we recite: "Blessed art Thou . . . who *creates* the lights of fire" (*Mishnah* Berachot 7,5) ; see Joseph Salomo Delmedigo, *Ta'alumot Hokmah, Nobelot Hokmah,* Basel, 1629, p. 94.